Meeting SEN
in the Curriculum:
SCIENCE

Other titles in the Meeting SEN in the Curriculum series:

Meeting SEN in the Curriculum:

SCIENCE

Carol Holden and Andy Cooke

David Fulton Publishers

David Fulton Publishers Ltd
The Chiswick Centre, 414 Chiswick High Road, London W4 5TF

www.fultonpublishers.co.uk

10 9 8 7 6 5 4 3 2 1

Note: the right of Carol Holden and Andy Cooke to be identified as the authors of this work
has been asserted by them in accordance with the Copyright, Designs and Patents Act 1988.

Copyright © Carol Holden and Andy Cooke 2005

British Library Cataloguing in Publication Data
A catalogue record for this book is available from the British Library.

David Fulton Publishers is a division of Granada Learning Limited, part of ITV plc.

ISBN 1 84312 159 X

Illustrations by Peter Stevenson

Typeset by Servis Filmsetting Ltd, Manchester
Printed and bound in Great Britain

Contents

Foreword

It is very pleasing to see a new publication that recognises the importance of addressing special educational needs in science and provides strategies for the classroom. Good practice and existing expertise need to be shared, and this book and CD provide valuable time-saving resources to support teachers and prevent them from having to 're-invent the wheel'. Effective collaboration has been advocated through ASE's collaborative work with NASEN over the last five years or more, and we are pleased to see this ethos reflected in this publication with reference to other sources of support, including our Inclusive Science website (www.issen.org.uk) and other outcomes from our work. Subject-specific publications addressing inclusion and special educational needs are extremely rare, as I have discovered from repeated visits to various special needs exhibitions, but there is a great need for contextualised support of this nature.

In using a publication such as this, it is noticeable that many of the strategies and inclusive approaches included can be helpful for science teachers in relation to working with *all* of their pupils, not just those with special educational needs. Good practice is good practice whatever the group of students, so ideas in this publication can be adapted and applied to improve teaching and learning for the majority of students. Teachers should not be concerned about where to start, or about having to implement lots of new strategies all at once. Dipping into this book and trying out just some of the ideas will help science teachers develop a better understanding of pupils' individual needs and enable them to create a more positive and stimulating learning environment.

Derek Bell (Chief Executive) and Adrian Fenton (Curriculum Support Manager),
Association for Science Education (www.ase.org.uk)

Adrian Fenton has been the Project Manager for the Inclusive Science project
between ASE and NASEN (National Association for Special Educational Needs)

Contributors to the Series

The authors

Carol Holden works as a science teacher and assistant SENCO in a mainstream secondary school. She has developed courses for pupils with SEN within science. Whilst continuing teaching, Carol has also gained a graduate diploma and MA in educational studies, focusing on SEN. As a result of Carol's interest in inclusion, she works closely with colleagues from local special schools, developing programmes involving pupils in studying science together.

Andy Cooke was a secondary science teacher for 14 years, during which time he was a key stage 3 science coordinator, head of physics and head of science. His experience includes teaching in a school with a specialist visually impaired unit. He is currently science adviser for Herefordshire. Other publications by Andy include Cambridge University Press's 'Spectrum' series.

Series editor

Alan Combes started teaching in South Yorkshire in 1967 and was head of English at several secondary schools before taking on the role of head of PSHE as part of being senior teacher at Pindar School, Scarborough. He took early retirement to focus on his writing career and has authored two citizenship textbooks as well as writing several features for the *TES*. He has been used as an adviser on citizenship by the DfES and a speaker for NASEN. **(SEN in Citizenship)**

A dedicated team of SEN specialists and subject specialists have contributed to the *Meeting SEN in the Curriculum* series.

SEN specialists

Sue Briggs is a freelance education consultant based in Hereford. She writes and speaks on inclusion, special educational needs and disability, and autistic spectrum disorders, and is a lay member of the SEN and Disability Tribunal. She was SEN inclusion coordinator for Herefordshire Education Directorate. Originally trained as a secondary music teacher, Sue has extensive experience in mainstream and special schools and was teacher in charge of a language disorder unit.

Sue Cunningham is a learning support coordinator at a large mainstream secondary school in the West Midlands where she manages a large team of learning support teachers and assistants. She has experience of working in both mainstream and special schools and has set up and managed a Resource Base for Pupils with Moderate Learning Difficulties in the mainstream.

Sally McKeown has responsibility for language-based work in the inclusion team at Becta. She has a particular interest in learning difficulties and dyslexia.

She wrote the MFL Special Needs Materials for CILT's NOF training and is author of *Unlocking Potential* and co-author of *Supporting Children with Dyslexia* (Questions Publishing). She writes regularly for the *TES, Guardian* and *Special Children* magazine.

Subject specialists

Religious Education

Dilwyn Hunt has been involved in teaching Religious Education for the last 30 years and has written a variety of popular textbooks. For the last 10 years he has worked as a specialist RE adviser, first in Birmingham and now in Dudley. He has a wide range of experience in the teaching of RE in both mainstream and special schools.

Maths

Brian Sharp is a key stage 3 mathematics consultant for Herefordshire, and has a long experience of working in both special and mainstream schools as a teacher of mathematics. He has a range of management experience, including SENCO, mathematics and ICT coordinator.

English

Tim Hurst has been a SENCO in five schools and is particularly interested in the role and use of language in teaching.

History

Richard Harris has been teaching since 1989. He has taught in three comprehensive schools, as history teacher, head of department and head of faculty. He has also worked as teacher consultant for secondary history in West Berkshire.

Ian Luff is assistant headteacher of Kesgrave High School, Suffolk and has been head of history in three comprehensive schools.

Design & Technology

Louise T. Davies is principal officer (part time) for design and technology at the Qualifications and Curriculum Authority and also a freelance consultant. She is an experienced presenter and author of award-winning resources and books for schools. She chairs the Special Needs Advisory Group for the Design and Technology Association.

Music

Victoria Jaquiss is SEN specialist for music for children with emotional and behavioural difficulties in Leeds. She devised a system of musical notation primarily for use with steel pans, for which, in 2002, she was awarded the fellowship of the Royal Society of Arts.

Diane Paterson works as an Inclusive Music Curriculum Teacher in Leeds.

Geography

Diane Swift is a project leader for the Geographical Association. Her interest in special needs developed whilst she was a Staffordshire geography adviser and inspector.

PE and Sport

Crispin Andrews is an education/sports writer with nine years' experience of teaching and sports coaching.

Art

Kim Earle is an adviser for St Helens and has been a head of art and design. Kim is also a practising designer jeweller.

Gill Curry has 20 years' experience as head of art and has also been an art advisory teacher. She is also a practising artist specialising in print.

ICT

Mike North works for ICTC, an independent consultancy specialising in the effective use of ICT in education. He develops educational materials and provides advice and support for the SEN sector.

Sally McKeown is an education officer with Becta, the government funded agency responsible for managing the National Grid for Learning and the FERL website. She is responsible for the use of ICT for learners with disabilities, learning difficulties or additional needs.

Citizenship

Alan Combes started teaching in South Yorkshire in 1967 and was head of English at several secondary schools before taking on the role of head of PSHE as part of being senior teacher at Pindar School, Scarborough. He took early retirement to focus on his writing career and has authored two citizenship textbooks as well as writing several features for the *TES*. He has been used as an adviser on citizenship by the DfES and has emphasised citizenship's importance for special needs pupils as a speaker for NASEN.

Modern Foreign Languages

Sally McKeown is responsible for language-based work in the inclusion team at Becta. She has a particular interest in learning difficulties and dyslexia. She writes regularly for the *TES*, *Guardian* and *Special Children* magazine.

Contents of the CD

The CD contains activities and record sheets that can be amended/individualised and printed out for use by the purchasing institution.

Please note that some of the images in the book have been included on the CD to allow readers to print out in full colour.

Increasing the font size and spacing will improve accessibility for some students, as will changes in background colour. Alternatively, print onto pastel-coloured paper for greater ease of reading.

1. INSET Activity: Main Points of SENDA — Appendix 2.1
2. INSET Activity: What Do We Really Think? — Appendix 2.2
3. Key Words for a Unit on Electricity — Appendix 4.1
4. Worksheet – Stopping Rust — Appendix 4.3
5. Writing Frame 1 – Planning an Investigation — Appendix 4.4
6. Presenting My Results — Appendix 4.5
7. Speaking Frame – A Science Experiment — Appendix 4.6
8. Number Line and Temperature Change — Appendix 4.7
9. Keeping a Tally — Appendix 4.8
10. Types of Numbers — Appendix 4.9
11. Time — Appendix 4.10
12. Measuring — Appendix 4.11
13. Thermometers Measure — Appendix 4.12
14. Boiling and Freezing — Appendix 4.13
15. Conductors and Insulators – Heat — Appendix 4.14
16. Conductors and Insulators – Electricity — Appendix 4.15
17. Reading Scales — Appendix 4.16
18. Graphs — Appendix 4.17
19. Entry Activity 1 – Wordsearch
20. Entry Activity 2 – Anagram
21. Entry Activity 3 – Diagram Labelling
22. Starter Activity 1 – Tug of War — Appendix 5.1
23. Starter Activity 2
24. DART Activity – True/False Exercise
25. Plenary Game – Dominoes
26. SMOG Test for Readability — Appendix 5.2
27. Homework Activity 1 – Learning Key Words — Appendix 5.3
28. Homework Activity 2 – Research — Appendix 5.3
29. Homework Activity 3 – Writing up an Experiment — Appendix 5.3
30. The 5-Star Lesson Plan — Appendix 5.4
31. Lesson Plan – Blank
32. Lesson Plan 1 – Control in Plants and Animals
33. Lesson Plan 2 – Compounds and Mixtures

Contents of the CD

xiv

Introduction

> All children have the right to a good education and the opportunity to fulfil their
> potential. All teachers should expect to teach children with special educational needs
> (SEN) and all schools should play their part in educating children from the local
> community, whatever their background or ability.
>
> (*Removing Barriers to Achievement: The Government's Strategy for SEN*, DfES 2004)

A raft of legislation and statutory guidance over the past few years has sought to
make our mainstream education system more inclusive and ensure that pupils
with a diverse range of ability and need are well catered for. This means that all
staff need to have an awareness of how children learn and develop in different
ways and an understanding of how barriers to achievement can be removed – or
at least minimised.

These barriers often result from inappropriate teaching styles, inaccessible
teaching materials or ill-advised grouping of pupils as much as from an
individual child's physical, sensory or cognitive impairments: a fact which is
becoming better understood. It is this developing understanding that is now
shaping the legislative and advisory landscape of our education system, and
exhorting all teachers to carefully consider their curriculum planning and
classroom practice.

The major statutory requirements and non-statutory guidance are
summarised in Chapter 1, setting the context for this resource and providing
useful starting points for departmental INSET.

It is clear that provision for pupils with special educational needs is not the
sole responsibility of the special educational needs coordinator (SENCO) and her
team of assistants. If, in the past, subject teachers have 'taken a back seat' in the
planning and delivery of a suitable curriculum for these children and expected
the Learning Support department to bridge the gap between what was on offer
in the classroom, lab or studio and what they actually needed, they can no longer
do so.

> All teaching and non-teaching staff should be involved in the development of
> the school's SEN policy and be fully aware of the school's procedure for
> identifying, assessing and making provision for pupils with SEN.
>
> (Table of roles and responsibilities, *SEN Code of Practice*, DfES 2001)

Chapter 2 looks at departmental policy for SEN provision and provides useful
audit material for reviewing and developing current practice.

The term 'special educational needs' or SEN is now widely used and has
become something of a catch-all descriptor – rendering it less than useful in
many cases. Before the Warnock Report (1978) and subsequent introduction of
the term 'special educational needs', any pupils who, for whatever reason
(cognitive difficulties, emotional and behavioural difficulties, speech and

language disorders), progressed more slowly than the 'norm' were designated 'remedials' and grouped together in the bottom sets, without the benefit, in many cases, of specialist subject teachers.

However, the SEN tag was also applied to pupils in special schools who had more significant needs and had previously been identified as 'disabled' or even 'uneducable'. Add to these the deaf pupils, those with impaired vision, others with mobility problems, and even children from other countries with a limited understanding of the English language – who may or may not have been highly intelligent – and you have a recipe for confusion, to say the least.

The day-to-day descriptors used in the staffroom are gradually being moderated and refined as greater knowledge and awareness of special needs is built up. (We still hear staff describing pupils as 'totally thick', a 'nutcase' or a 'complete moron' – but, we hope, only as a means of letting off steam!) However, there are terms in common use which, though more measured and well-meaning, can still be unhelpful and misleading. Teachers will describe a child as being 'dyslexic' when they mean that he is poor at reading and writing; 'ADHD' (attention deficit hyperactivity disorder) has become a synonym for badly behaved, and a child who seems to be withdrawn or just eccentric is increasingly described as 'autistic'.

The whole process of applying labels is fraught with danger but sharing a common vocabulary – and, more importantly, a common understanding – can help colleagues to express their concerns about a pupil and address the issues as they arise in the science lab. Often, this is better achieved by identifying the particular areas of difficulty experienced by the pupil rather than puzzling over what syndrome he may have. The *SEN Code of Practice* identifies four main areas of difficulty and these are detailed in Chapter 3 – along with an 'at a glance' guide to a wide range of syndromes and conditions and guidance on how they might present barriers to learning.

There is no doubt that the number of children with special needs being educated in mainstream schools is growing:

> . . . because of the increased emphasis on the inclusion of children with SEN in mainstream schools the number of these children is increasing, as are the severity and variety of their SEN. Children with a far wider range of learning difficulties and variety of medical conditions, as well as sensory difficulties and physical disabilities, are now attending mainstream classes. The implication of this is that mainstream school teachers need to expand their knowledge and skills with regard to the needs of children with SEN.
>
> (Stakes and Hornby 2000:3)

The continuing move to greater inclusion means that all teachers can now expect to teach pupils with varied, and quite significant, special educational needs at some time. Even five years ago, it was rare to come across children with Asperger/Down/Tourette syndrome, autistic spectrum disorders or significant physical/sensory disabilities in community secondary schools. Now, such children are entering mainstream education in growing numbers and there is a realisation that their 'inclusion' cannot be simply the responsibility of the

SENCO and support staff. All staff have to be aware of particular learning needs and be able to employ strategies in the classroom and science lab that directly address those needs.

Chapter 4 considers the components of an inclusive setting and how the physical environment and resources, structure of the lesson and teaching approaches can make a real difference to pupils with special needs. This theme is extended in Chapter 5 to look more closely at teaching and learning styles and to consider ways in which to help all pupils maximise their potential.

The monitoring of pupils' achievements and progress is a key factor in identifying and meeting their learning needs. Those pupils who make slower progress than their peers are often working just as hard, or even harder, but their efforts can go unrewarded. Chapter 6 addresses the importance of target setting and subsequent assessment and review in acknowledging pupils' achievements and in showing the department's effectiveness in value-added terms.

Liaising with the SENCO and support staff is an important part of every teacher's role. The SENCO's status in a secondary school often means that she is part of the leadership team and influential in shaping whole-school policy and practice; specific duties might include:

- ensuring liaison with parents and other professionals

- advising and supporting teaching and support staff

- ensuring that appropriate Individual Education Plans (IEPs) are in place

- ensuring that relevant background information about individual children with special educational needs is collected, recorded and updated

- making plans for future support and setting targets for improvement

- monitoring and reviewing action taken.

The SENCO has invariably undergone training in various aspects of special needs provision and has much to offer colleagues in terms of in-house training and advice about appropriate materials to use with pupils. She should be a frequent and valuable point of reference for all staff, but is often overlooked in this capacity. Her presence at the occasional departmental meeting can be very effective in developing teachers' skills in relation to meeting SEN, making them aware of new initiatives and methodology, and sharing information about individual children.

In most schools, however, the SENCO's skills and knowledge are channelled to the chalkface via a team of teaching or learning support assistants (TAs, LSAs). These assistants can be very able and well-qualified, but very underused in the classroom. Chapter 7 looks at how teachers can manage in-class support in a way that makes the best use of a valuable resource.

Describing real-life situations with real pupils is a powerful way to demonstrate ideas and guidance. In Chapter 8, a number of case studies illustrate how different approaches can work.

The revised regulations for SEN provision make it clear that mainstream schools are expected to provide for pupils with a wide diversity of needs, and science teaching is evaluated on the extent to which all pupils are engaged and enabled to achieve.

> Inclusive science involves issues of access, quality, relevance and purpose . . . all students with special educational needs are entitled to access to high-quality science education that recognises and responds to diverse learning needs. The nature of science presents first-hand experiences including practical activity, which can enliven the imagination and has the potential to enable all learners to achieve success. Active learning within the science curriculum can also facilitate the development of interpersonal communication and self-advocacy, and contribute to enhancing the self-esteem of the learners.
>
> (ASE/NASEN joint statement, November 2002)

This book has been produced in response to the implications of all of this for science teachers in mainstream secondary schools. It has been written by subject specialists with support from colleagues who have expertise within the SEN field so that the information and guidance given is both subject-specific and pedagogically sound. The book and accompanying CD provide a resource that can be used with colleagues:

- to shape departmental policy and practice for special needs provision

- to enable staff to react with a measured response when inclusion issues arise

- to ensure that every pupil achieves appropriately in science.

CHAPTER 1

Meeting Special Educational Needs – Your Responsibility

Inclusion in education involves the process of increasing the participation of students in, and reducing their exclusion from, the cultures, curricula and communities of local schools.

(Booth *et al.*, 2000)

The *Index for Inclusion* was distributed to all maintained schools by the Department for Education and Skills and has been a valuable tool for many schools as they have worked to develop their inclusive practice. It supports schools in the review of their policies, practices and procedures and the development of an inclusive approach, and, where it has been used as part of the school improvement process – looking at inclusion in the widest sense – it has been a great success. For many people, however, the *Index* lacked any real teeth and recent legislation and non-statutory guidance is more authoritative.

The SEN and Disability Act 2001 (SENDA)

The Act amended the Disability Discrimination Act and created important new duties for schools:

- to take reasonable steps to ensure that disabled pupils are not placed at a substantial disadvantage in relation to the education and other services they provide. This means they must anticipate where barriers to learning lie and take action to remove them as far as they are able.

- to plan strategically to increase the extent to which disabled pupils can participate in the curriculum, make the physical environment more accessible, and ensure that written material is provided in accessible formats.

The reasonable steps taken might include:

- changing policies and practices
- changing course requirements

- changing physical features of a building

- providing interpreters or other support workers

- delivering courses in alternative ways

- providing materials in other formats

- having adapted apparatus

- providing suitable alternative activities.

(The staff in one science department produce all their materials in electronic form to ensure that they can easily be converted into large print or put into other alternative formats, such as Braille. They are anticipating 'reasonable adjustments' that might need to be made.)

See Chapter 2 for further detail on SENDA and an INSET activity.

The revised National Curriculum

The revised National Curriculum (2002) emphasises the provision of effective learning opportunities for all learners and establishes three principles for promoting inclusion:

- the setting of suitable learning challenges

- responding to pupils' diverse learning needs

- overcoming potential barriers to learning and assessment.

The National Curriculum guidance suggests that staff may need to differentiate tasks and materials, and facilitate access to learning by:

- encouraging pupils to use all available senses and experiences

- planning for participation in all activities

- helping children to manage their behaviour, take part in learning and prepare for work

- helping pupils to manage their emotions

- giving teachers, where necessary, the discretion to teach pupils material from earlier key stages, providing consideration is given to age-appropriate learning context.

This means that a fourteen-year-old with significant learning difficulties may be taught relevant aspects of the programmes of study for science at key stage 3, but adapted to a level of achievement below that usually expected at key stage 3. The important underlying principle must be that the context of the activity is age-appropriate even if the expected outcome is in line with National Curriculum level 1 or a P level.

The Qualifications and Curriculum Authority (QCA) have introduced performance descriptions (P levels/P scales) to enable teachers to observe and record small steps of progress made by some pupils with SEN. These descriptions outline early learning and attainment for each subject in the National Curriculum. They chart progress up to National Curriculum level 1 through eight steps. The performance descriptions for P1 to P3 are common across all subjects and outline the types and range of general performance that some pupils with significant learning difficulties might characteristically demonstrate. From level P4, many believe it is possible to describe performance in a way that indicates the emergence of subject-focused skills, knowledge and understanding. (See Chapter 6.)

The Code of Practice for Special Educational Needs

The revised *SEN Code of Practice* (implemented in 2002) describes a cyclical process of planning, target setting and review for pupils with special educational needs. It also makes clear the expectation that the vast majority of pupils with special needs will be educated in mainstream settings. Those identified as needing over and above what the school can provide from its own resources, however, are nominated for 'School Action Plus' and outside agencies will be involved in planned intervention. This may involve professionals from the Learning Support Service, a specialist teacher or therapist, or an educational psychologist, working with the school's special educational needs coordinator (SENCO) to put together an Individual Education Plan (IEP) for the pupil. In a minority of cases (the numbers vary widely between local authorities (LAs)), pupils may be assessed by a multidisciplinary team on behalf of the LA. Their representatives then decide whether or not to issue a Statement of SEN. This is a legally binding document detailing the child's needs and setting out the resources which should be provided. It is reviewed every year.

FUNDAMENTAL PRINCIPLES OF THE SPECIAL EDUCATIONAL NEEDS CODE OF PRACTICE:

- A child with special educational needs should have their needs met

- The special educational needs of children will normally be met in mainstream schools or settings

- The views of the child should be sought and taken into account

- Parents have a vital role to play in supporting their child's education

- Children with special educational needs should be offered full access to a broad, balanced and relevant education, including an appropriate curriculum for the foundation stage and the National Curriculum.

Ofsted

Ofsted inspectors are required to make judgements about a school's inclusion policy, and how this is translated into practice in individual classrooms. According to Ofsted (2003), the following key factors help schools to become more inclusive:

- a climate of acceptance of all pupils

- careful preparation of placements for SEN pupils

- availability of sufficient suitable teaching and personal support

- widespread awareness among staff of the particular needs of SEN pupils and an understanding of the practical ways of meeting these needs in the classroom

- sensitive allocation to teaching groups and careful curriculum modification, timetables and social arrangements

- availability of appropriate materials and teaching aids and adapted accommodation

- an active approach to personal and social development (PSD), as well as to learning

- well-defined and consistently applied approaches to managing difficult behaviour

- assessment, recording and reporting procedures which can embrace and express adequately the progress of pupils with more complex SEN who make only small gains in learning and Personal and Social Development

- involving parents/carers as fully as possible in decision-making, keeping them well-informed about their child's progress and giving them as much practical support as possible

- developing and taking advantage of training opportunities, including links with special schools and other schools.

Policy into practice

Effective teaching for pupils with special educational needs is, by and large, effective for all pupils but, as schools become more inclusive, teachers need to be able to respond to a wider range of needs. The Government's strategy for SEN, *Removing Barriers to Achievement* (DfES 2004), sets out ambitious proposals to 'help teachers expand their repertoire of inclusive skills and strategies and plan confidently to include children with increasingly complex needs'.

In many cases, pupils' individual needs will be met through greater differentiation of tasks and materials, i.e. school-based intervention as set out in the *SEN Code of Practice*. A smaller number of pupils may need access to specialist equipment and approaches, or to alternative or adapted activities, as part of a 'School Action Plus' programme, augmented by advice and support from external specialists. The QCA give the following guidance on their website (2003):

Teachers are encouraged to take specific action to provide access to learning for pupils with special educational needs by:

(a) providing for pupils who need help with communication, language and literacy, through:

- using texts that pupils can read and understand
- using visual and written materials in different formats, including large print, symbol text and Braille
- using ICT, other technological aids and taped materials
- using alternative and augmentative communication, including signs and symbols
- using translators, communicators and amanuenses.

(b) planning, where necessary, to develop pupils' understanding through the use of all available senses and experiences:

- using materials and resources that pupils can access through sight, touch, sound, taste or smell
- using word descriptions and other stimuli to make up for a lack of first-hand experiences
- using ICT, visual and other materials to increase pupils' knowledge of the wider world
- encouraging pupils to take part in everyday activities such as play, drama, class visits and exploring the environment.

(c) planning for pupils' full participation in learning and in physical and practical activities:

- using specialist aids and equipment
- providing support from adults or peers when needed
- adapting tasks, equipment or environments
- providing alternative activities, where necessary.

(d) helping pupils to manage their behaviour, to take part in learning effectively and safely, and, at key stage 4, to prepare for work:

- setting realistic demands and stating them explicitly
- using positive behaviour management, including a clear structure of rewards and sanctions

- giving pupils every chance and encouragement to develop the skills they need to work well with a partner or a group

- teaching pupils to value and respect the contribution of others

- encouraging and teaching independent working skills

- teaching essential safety rules.

(e) helping individuals to manage their emotions, particularly trauma or stress, and to take part in learning:

- identifying aspects of learning in which the pupil will engage and plan short-term, easily achievable goals in selected activities

- providing positive feedback to reinforce and encourage learning and build self-esteem

- selecting tasks and materials sensitively to avoid unnecessary stress for the pupil

- creating a supportive learning environment in which the pupil feels safe and is able to engage with learning

- allowing time for the pupil to engage with learning and gradually increasing the range of activities and demands

- health and safety issues are an important consideration in science; for example, it is usually not appropriate for pupils to 'taste' in the laboratory. Some practical activities may be unsafe unless pupils can have one-to-one support.

Pupils with disabilities

Not all pupils with disabilities will necessarily have special educational needs. Many learn alongside their peers with little need for additional resources beyond the aids which they use as part of their daily life, such as a wheelchair, a hearing aid or equipment to aid vision. Teachers' planning must ensure, however, that these pupils are enabled to participate as fully and effectively as possible in the curriculum by:

(a) planning appropriate amounts of time to allow for the satisfactory completion of tasks, which might involve:

- adapting apparatus (e.g. white or coloured tape around the lip of a beaker for students with visual impairments)

- taking account of the very slow pace at which some pupils will be able to record work, either manually or with specialist equipment, and of the physical effort required

- being aware of the high levels of concentration necessary for some pupils when following or interpreting text or graphics, particularly when using vision aids or tactile methods, and of the tiredness which may result

- allocating sufficient time, opportunity and access to equipment for pupils to gain information through experimental work and detailed observation, including the use of microscopes

- being aware of the effort required by some pupils to follow oral work, whether through use of residual hearing, lip reading or a signer, and of the tiredness or loss of concentration which may occur.

(b) planning opportunities, where necessary, for the development of skills in practical aspects of the curriculum, which might involve:

- providing alternative or adapted activities in science, for pupils who are unable to manipulate equipment or materials or who may be allergic to certain types of materials

- ensuring that all pupils can be included and participate safely in field work.

(c) identifying aspects of programmes of study and attainment targets that may present specific difficulties for individuals, which might involve:

- using adapted approaches to enable hearing-impaired pupils to learn about sound and helping visually impaired pupils to learn about light.

Conclusion

Teachers are ultimately responsible for all the children they teach. In terms of participation, achievement, enjoyment, the buck stops here!

Pupils with a wide range of needs – physical/sensory, emotional, cognitive and social – are present in increasing numbers, in all mainstream settings.

Government policies point the way, with inclusion at the forefront of national policy, but it is up to teachers to make the rhetoric a reality.

Chapter 2 considers the departmental policy for special educational needs provision and inclusion, and how its development can shape classroom practice.

Departmental Policy

It is crucial that departmental policy describes a strategy for meeting pupils' special educational needs within the particular curricular area. The policy should set the scene for any visitor to the science department – from supply staff to inspectors – and make a valuable contribution to the departmental handbook. The process of developing a department SEN policy offers the opportunity to clarify and evaluate current thinking and practice within the science team and to establish a consistent approach.

The policy should:

- clarify the responsibilities of all staff and identify any with specialist training and/or knowledge

- describe the curriculum on offer and how it can be differentiated

- outline arrangements for assessment and reporting

- guide staff on how to work effectively with support staff

- identify staff training needs.

The starting point will be the school's SEN policy as required by the Education Act 1996, with each subject department 'fleshing out' the detail in a way which describes how things work in practice. The writing of a policy should be much more than a paper exercise completed to satisfy the senior management team and Ofsted inspectors: it is an opportunity for staff to come together as a team and create a framework for teaching science in a way that makes it accessible to all pupils in the school.

Where to start when writing a policy?

An audit can act as a starting point for reviewing current policy on SEN or to inform the writing of a new policy. It will involve gathering information and reviewing current practice with regard to pupils with SEN and is best completed by the whole of the department, preferably with some additional advice from the SENCO or another member of staff with responsibility for SEN within the school. An audit carried out by the whole department can provide a valuable opportunity for professional development if it is seen as an exercise in sharing good practice and encouraging joint planning. However, before embarking on an audit it is worth investing some time in a department meeting or training day, to raise awareness of special educational needs legislation and to establish a shared philosophy. Appendices 2.1 and 2.2 contain OHT layouts and an activity to use with staff. (These are also on the accompanying CD, with additional exercises you may choose to use.)

Useful headings when establishing a working policy

General statement

- What does legislation and DfES guidance say?
- What does the school policy state?
- What do members of the department have to do to comply with it?

Definition of SEN

- What does SEN mean?
- What are the areas of need and the categories used in the *SEN Code of Practice*?
- Are there any special implications within the subject area?

Provision for staff within the department

- How is information shared?
- Who has responsibility for SEN within the department?
- How and when is information shared?
- Where and what information is stored?

Provision for pupils with SEN

- How are pupils with SEN assessed and monitored in the department?
- How are contributions to IEPs and reviews made?
- What criteria are used for organising teaching groups?
- What alternative courses are offered to pupils with SEN?
- What special internal and external examination arrangements are made?
- What guidance is available for working with support staff?

Resources and learning materials

- Is there any specialist equipment used in the department?

- How are resources developed?

- Where are resources stored?

Staff qualifications and continuing professional development needs

- What qualifications do the members of the department have?

- What training has taken place?

- How is training planned?

- Is a record kept of training completed and training needs?

Monitoring and reviewing the policy

- How will the policy be monitored?

- When will the policy be reviewed?

The content of a science departmental policy for SEN

This section gives detailed information on what an SEN policy might include. Each heading is expanded with some detailed information and raises the main issues with regard to teaching pupils with SEN. At the end of each section there is an examplar statement. These statements can be personalised and brought together to make a policy.

General statement with reference to the school's SEN policy

All schools must have an SEN policy according to the Education Act 1996. This policy will set out basic information on the school's SEN provision, and how the school identifies, assesses and provides for pupils with SEN, including information on staffing and working in partnership with other professionals and parents.

Any departmental policy needs to have reference to the school SEN policy.

Example

> All members of the department will ensure that the needs of all pupils with SEN are met, according to the aims of the school and its SEN policy.

Definition of SEN

It is useful to insert at least the four areas of SEN in the departmental policy, as used in the *SEN Code of Practice.*

THE FOUR AREAS OF SEN

Cognition and Learning Needs	Behavioural, Emotional and Social Development Needs	Communication and Interaction Needs	Sensory and/or Physical Needs
Specific Learning Difficulties (SpLD) Dyslexia Dyscalculia Dyspraxia	Behavioural, Emotional and Social Difficulties (BESD)	Speech, Language and Communication Needs	Hearing Impairment (HI)
Down syndrome Fragile X syndrome	Attention Deficit Disorder (ADD)	Autistic Spectrum Disorders (ASD)	Visual Impairment (VI)
Moderate Learning Difficulties (MLD)	Attention Deficit Hyperactivity Disorder (ADHD)	Asperger syndrome	Multi-Sensory Impairment (MSI)
Severe Learning Difficulties (SLD)		Semantic Pragmatic Disorder (SPD)	Cerebral palsy Physical Difficulties (PD)
Profound and Multiple Learning Difficulties (PMLD)			Tourette syndrome

Provision for staff within the department

In many schools, each department nominates a member of staff to have special responsibility for SEN provision (with or without remuneration). This can be very effective where there is a system of regular liaison between department SEN representatives and the SENCO in the form of meetings or paper communications, or a mixture of both.

The responsibilities of this post may include liaison between the department and the SENCO, attending any liaison meetings and providing feedback via meetings and minutes, attending training, maintaining the departmental SEN information and records, and representing the needs of pupils with SEN at departmental level. This post can be seen as a valuable development opportunity for staff. The name of this person should be included in the policy.

Setting out how members of the department raise concerns about pupils with SEN can be included in this section. Concerns may be raised at specified departmental meetings before referral to the SENCO. An identified member of the department could make referrals to the SENCO and keep a record of this information.

Reference to working with support staff will include a commitment to planning and communication between staff. There may be information on inviting support staff to meetings, resources and lesson plans.

A reference to the centrally held lists of pupils with SEN and other relevant information will also be included in this section. A note about confidentiality of information should be included.

Example

> The member of staff with responsibility for overseeing the provision of SEN within the department will attend liaison meetings and feed back to other members of the department. He will maintain the department's SEN information file, attend appropriate training and disseminate this to all departmental staff. All information will be treated with confidentiality.

Provision for pupils with SEN

It is the responsibility of all staff to know which pupils have SEN and to identify any pupils having difficulties. Pupils with SEN may be identified by staff within the department in a variety of ways; these may be listed and could include:

- observation in lessons, especially when completing practical work

- assessment of class work

- homework tasks

- end-of-module tests

- progress checks

- annual examinations

- reports.

Setting out how pupils with SEN are grouped within the science department may include specifying the criteria used and/or the philosophy behind the method of grouping.

Example

> The pupils are grouped according to ability as informed by key stage 2 results, reading scores and any other relevant performance, social or medical information.

Monitoring arrangements and details of how pupils can move between groups should also be set out. Information collected may include:

- National Curriculum levels

- departmental assessments

- reading scores

- advice from pastoral staff

- discussion with staff in the SEN department

- information provided on IEPs.

Special examination arrangements need to be considered not only at key stages 3 and 4 but also for internal examinations. How and when these will be discussed should be clarified. Reference to SENCO and examination arrangements from the examination board should be taken into account. Recognition that staff in the department understand the current legislation and guidance from central government is important so a reference to the *SEN Code of Practice* and the levels of SEN intervention is helpful within the policy. Here is a good place also to put a statement about the school behaviour policy and rewards and sanctions, and how the department will make any necessary adjustments to meet the needs of pupils with SEN.

With reference to the interface between the school behaviour policy and the special considerations of the science department, it is preferable to adopt an active and positive approach. An atmosphere created from rewarding pupils who have a sound working knowledge of how to conduct oneself in a laboratory situation will pay obvious dividends.

Example

It is understood that pupils with SEN may receive additional support if they have a Statement of SEN, are at School Action Plus or School Action. The staff in the science department will aim to support the pupils to achieve their targets as specified on their IEPs and will provide feedback for IEP or Statement reviews. Pupils with SEN will be included in the departmental monitoring system used for all pupils. Additional support will be requested as appropriate.

Resources and learning materials

The departmental policy needs to specify what differentiated materials are available, where they are kept and how to find new resources. This section could include a statement about working with support staff to develop resources or to access specialist resources as needed and the use of ICT. Teaching strategies may also be identified if appropriate. Advice on more specialist equipment can be sought as necessary, possibly through LEA support services: contact details may be available from the SENCO, or the department may have direct links.

Any specially bought subject text or alternative/appropriate courses can be specified, as well as any external assessment and examination courses.

Example

> The department will provide suitably differentiated materials and, where appropriate, specialist resources for pupils with SEN. Additional texts are available for those pupils working below National Curriculum level 3. At key stage 4 an alternative course to GCSE is offered at Entry level, but where possible pupils with SEN will be encouraged to reach their full potential and follow a GCSE course. Support staff will be provided with curriculum information in advance of lessons and will also be involved in lesson planning. A list of resources is available in the department handbook and on the noticeboard.

Staff qualifications and Continuing Professional Development needs

It is important to recognise and record the qualifications and special skills gained by staff within the department. Training can include not only external courses but also in-house INSET and opportunities such as observing other staff, working to produce materials jointly, and visiting other establishments. Staff may have hidden skills that might enhance the work of the department and the school: for example, some staff might be proficient in the use of sign language.

Example

> A record of training undertaken, specialist skills and training required will be kept in the department handbook. Requests for training will be considered in line with the department and school improvement plan.

Monitoring and reviewing the policy

Any policy that is to be effective needs regular monitoring and review. These can be planned as part of the annual cycle. The responsibility for the monitoring can rest with the head of department but will have more effect if supported by someone from outside acting as a critical friend – this could be the SENCO or a member of the senior management team in the school.

Example

> The departmental SEN policy will be monitored by the head of department on a planned annual basis, with advice being sought from the SENCO as part of a three-yearly review process.

Conclusion

Creating a departmental SEN policy should be a developmental activity to improve the teaching and learning for all pupils but especially those with special or additional needs. The policy should be a working document that will evolve and change; it is there to challenge current practice and to encourage improvement for both pupils and staff. If departmental staff work together to create the policy, they will have ownership of it; it will have true meaning and be effective in clarifying practice.

(OHT sheets of the main points in SENDA and of staff INSET activities are included in the appendices and on the accompanying CD.)

CHAPTER 3

Different Types of SEN

This chapter is a starting point for information on the special educational needs most frequently occurring in the mainstream secondary school. It describes the main characteristics of each learning difficulty along with practical ideas for use in science lessons and contacts for further information. Some of the tips are based on good secondary practice whilst others encourage teachers to try new or less familiar approaches.

The special educational needs in this chapter are grouped under the headings used in the *SEN Code of Practice* (DfES 2001):

- cognition and learning needs

- behavioural, emotional and social development needs

- communication and interaction needs

- sensory and/or physical needs.

The labels used in this chapter are useful when describing pupils' difficulties but it is important to remember not to use the label in order to define the pupil. Put the pupil before the difficulty, saying, 'the pupil with special educational needs' rather than 'the SEN pupil', 'pupils with MLD' rather than 'MLDs'.

Remember to take care in using labels when talking with parents, pupils or other professionals. Unless a pupil has a firm diagnosis, and parents and pupil understand the implications of that diagnosis, it is more appropriate to describe the features of the special educational need rather than use the label. For example, a teacher might describe a pupil's spelling difficulties but not use the term 'dyslexic'.

The number and profile of pupils with special educational needs will vary from school to school, so it is important to consider the pupil with SEN as an individual within your school and subject environment. The strategies contained in this chapter will help teachers adapt that environment to meet the needs of individual pupils within the subject context. For example, rather than saying, 'He can't read the worksheet', recognise that the worksheet is too difficult for the pupil, and adapt the work accordingly.

There is a continuum of need within each of the special educational needs listed here. Some pupils will be affected more than others, and show fewer or more of the characteristics described.

The availability and levels of support from professionals within a school (e.g. SENCOs, support teachers, teaching assistants) and external professionals (e.g. educational psychologists, Learning Support Service staff, medical staff) will depend on the severity of pupils' SEN. This continuum of need will also impact on the science teacher's planning and allocation of support staff.

Pupils with other less common special educational needs may be included in some secondary schools, and additional information on these conditions may be found in a variety of sources. These include the school SENCO, LA support services, educational psychologists and the internet.

COGNITION AND LEARNING NEEDS

Specific learning difficulties (SpLD)

The term 'specific learning difficulties' covers dyslexia, dyscalculia and dyspraxia.

Dyslexia

The term 'dyslexia' is used to describe a learning difficulty associated with words and it can affect a pupil's ability to read, write and/or spell. Research has shown that there is no one definitive definition of dyslexia or one identified cause and it has a wide range of symptoms. Although it is found across a whole range of ability levels, the idea that dyslexia presents as a difference between expected outcomes and performance is widely held. Pupils with dyslexia often also have difficulties with remembering things, and with personal organisation.

Main characteristics

- **Reading**
  The pupil may frequently lose their place, make a lot of errors with the high-frequency words, have difficulty reading names, and have difficulty blending sounds and segmenting words. Reading requires a great deal of effort and concentration.

- **Writing**
  The pupil's work may seem messy with crossing outs, similarly shaped letters such as b/d/p/q, m/w, n/u may be confused and letters in words may be jumbled: tired/tried. Spelling difficulties often persist into adult life and these pupils become reluctant writers.

How can the science teacher help?

- Be aware of the type of difficulty and the pupil's strengths.

- Teach and allow the use of word processing, spell checkers and computer-aided learning packages.

- Provide word lists and photocopies of copying from the board.

- Consider alternative recording methods, e.g. pictures, plans, flow charts, mind maps.

- Allow extra time for tasks including assessments and examinations.

The British Dyslexia Association
Tel: 0118 966 8271, website: www.bda-dyslexia.org.uk

The Dyslexia Institute
Tel: 07184 463 851, website: www.dyslexia-inst.org.uk

Dyscalculia

The term 'dyscalculia' is used to describe a difficulty in mathematics. This might be either a marked discrepancy between the pupil's developmental level and general ability on measures of specific maths ability or a total inability to abstract or consider concepts and numbers.

Main characteristics

- **Numbers**
  The pupil may have difficulty counting by rote, writing or reading numbers, miss out or reverse numbers, have difficulty with mental maths, and be unable to remember concepts, rules and formulae.

- **Maths-based concepts**
  The pupil may have difficulty with measurements, telling the time, directions, right and left, sequencing events or losing track of turns, e.g. in team games.

How can the science teacher help?

- Provide number/word/rule/formulae lists and photocopies of copying from the board.

- Make use of ICT and teach the use of calculators.

- Encourage the use of rough paper for working out.

- Plan the setting out of work with it well spaced on the page.

- Provide practical objects that are age appropriate to aid recording of data (keeping a tally, etc.).

- Allow extra time for tasks including assessments and examinations.

www.dyscalculia.co.uk

Dyspraxia

The term 'dyspraxia' is used to describe an immaturity with the way in which the brain processes information, resulting in messages not being properly transmitted. It is usually associated with coordination difficulties but can also affect the way that children think.

Main characteristics

- difficulty in coordinating movements, may appear awkward and clumsy
- difficulty with handwriting, drawing, using apparatus in practical work
- difficulty following sequential events, e.g. multiple instructions
- may misinterpret situations, take things literally
- limited social skills and may become frustrated and irritable
- some articulation difficulties (verbal dyspraxia).

How can the science teacher help?

- Be sensitive to the pupil's limitations in practical work, and plan tasks to enable success.
- Consider the use of adapted equipment.
- Ask the pupil questions to check their understanding of instructions/tasks.
- Check seating position to encourage good presentation of written work (lab stools and benches may not be ideal, which would be both feet resting on the floor, desk at elbow height and with a sloping surface to work on).

The Dyspraxia Foundation
Tel: 01462 454 986, website: www.dyspraxiafoundation.org.uk

Down syndrome

Down syndrome is the most common identifiable cause of learning disability. This is a genetic condition caused by the presence of an extra chromosome 21. People with Down syndrome have varying degrees of learning difficulties ranging from mild to severe. They have a specific learning profile with characteristic strengths and weaknesses. All share certain physical characteristics but will also inherit family traits, in physical features and personality. They may have additional sight, hearing, respiratory and heart problems.

Main characteristics

- delayed motor skills
- take longer to learn and consolidate new skills
- limited concentration
- difficulties with generalisation, thinking and reasoning
- sequencing difficulties
- stronger visual than aural skills
- better social than academic skills.

How can the science teacher help?

- Sit the pupil where they are best able to see and hear.
- Speak directly to the pupil and reinforce with facial expression, pictures and objects.
- Use simple, familiar language in short sentences – explain new vocabulary and encourage the pupil to use simple dictionaries and word banks.
- Check that instructions have been understood.
- Allow time to process information and formulate a response.
- Break lessons up into a series of shorter, varied and achievable tasks.
- Accept varied ways of recording: drawings, tape/video recordings, symbols, etc.
- Set differentiated tasks linked to the work of the rest of the class.
- Provide age-appropriate resources and activities.
- Allow working in top sets to give good behaviour models.
- Provide a work buddy.
- Expect unsupported work for part of each lesson.

Down's Syndrome Association
Tel: 020 8682 4001, website: www.downs-syndrome.org.uk

Fragile X syndrome

Fragile X syndrome is caused by a malformation of the X chromosome and is the most common form of inherited learning disability. This intellectual disability varies widely with up to a third having learning problems ranging from moderate to severe. More boys than girls are affected but both may be carriers.

Main characteristics

- delayed and disordered speech and language development
- difficulties with the social use of language
- articulation and/or fluency difficulties
- verbal skills better developed than reasoning skills
- repetitive or obsessive behaviour such as hand-flapping, chewing, etc.
- clumsiness and fine motor coordination problems
- attention deficit and hyperactivity
- easily anxious or overwhelmed in busy environments.

How can the science teacher help?

- Make sure the pupil knows what is to happen in each lesson – visual timetables, work schedules or written lists.
- Sit the pupil at the front of the lab, in the same place for all lessons.
- Arrange a work/subject buddy.
- Where possible, keep to routines and give prior warning of all changes.
- Make instructions clear and simple.
- Use visual supports: objects, pictures, symbols, etc.
- Have a class science dictionary and/or word bank compiled in simple language – refer to it throughout the lesson.
- Allow the pupil to use a computer to record and access information.
- Give lots of praise and positive feedback.

The Fragile X Society
Tel: 01434 813 147 (helpline), 01371 875 100 (office)
Email: info@fragilex.org.uk, website: www.fragilex.org.uk

Moderate learning difficulties (MLD)

The term 'moderate learning difficulties' is used to describe pupils who find it extremely difficult to achieve expected levels of attainment across the curriculum even with a differentiated and flexible approach. These pupils do not find learning easy and can suffer from low self-esteem and sometimes exhibit unacceptable behaviour as a way of avoiding failure.

Main characteristics

- difficulties with reading, writing and comprehension
- unable to understand and retain basic science skills and concepts
- immature social and emotional skills
- limited vocabulary and communication skills
- short attention span
- under-developed coordination skills
- lack of logical reasoning
- inability to transfer and apply skills to different situations
- difficulty remembering what has been taught
- difficulty with organising themselves, following a timetable, remembering books and equipment.

How can the science teacher help?

- Check the pupil's strengths, weaknesses and attainment levels.
- Establish a routine within the lesson – starter, main and plenary sessions.
- Keep tasks short and varied.
- Keep listening tasks short or broken up with activities.
- Provide word lists, simple science dictionaries, writing frames.
- Try alternative methods of recording information, e.g. drawings, charts, labelling, diagrams, use of ICT (e.g. Clicker software).
- Check previously gained knowledge and build on this.
- Repeat information in different ways – use a VAK approach (visual, auditory, kinaesthetic) to utilise all the senses.
- Show the child what to do or what the expected outcome is, demonstrate or show examples of completed work.

- Use practical, concrete, visual examples to illustrate explanations.

- Question the pupil to check they have grasped a concept or can follow instructions.

- Make sure the pupil always has something to do.

- Use lots of praise, instant rewards, catch them trying hard.

The MLD Alliance
Tel: 020 7359 7443, website: www.mldalliance.com/executive.htm

Severe learning difficulties

The term 'severe learning difficulties' covers a wide and varied group of pupils who have significant intellectual or cognitive impairments. Many have communication difficulties and/or sensory impairments in addition to more general cognitive impairments. They may also have difficulties in mobility, coordination and perception. Some pupils may use signs and symbols to support their communication and understanding. Their attainments may be within or below level 1 of the National Curriculum, or in the upper P scale range (P4–P8), for much of their school careers.

How can the science teacher help?

- Arrange a work/subject buddy.

- Use visual supports: objects, pictures, symbols.

- Learn some signs relevant to the subject.

- Allow time to process information and formulate responses.

- Set differentiated tasks linked to the work of the rest of the class.

- Set achievable targets for each lesson or module of work.

- Accept different recording methods: drawings, audio or video recordings, photographs, etc.

- Give access to computers where appropriate.

- Give a series of short, varied activities within each lesson.

Profound and multiple learning difficulties (PMLD)

Pupils with 'profound and multiple learning difficulties' (PMLD) have complex learning needs. In addition to very severe learning difficulties, pupils have other significant difficulties, such as physical disabilities, sensory impairments or severe medical conditions. Pupils with PMLD require a high level of adult support, both for their learning needs and for their personal care.

They are able to access the curriculum through sensory experiences and stimulation. Some pupils communicate by gesture, eye pointing or symbols, others by very simple language. Their attainments are likely to remain in the early P scale range (P1–P4) throughout their school careers (that is, below level 1 of the National Curriculum). The P scales provide small, achievable steps to monitor progress. Some pupils will make no progress or may even regress because of associated medical conditions. For this group, experiences are as important as attainment.

Where these pupils are welcomed into mainstream schools, it is often on a part-time basis. Liaison with staff from the special school or setting will be valuable in enabling the science teacher to plan appropriate work and formulate appropriate expectations.

How can the science teacher help?

- Liaise with parents and teaching assistants.

- Consider the classroom layout.

- Identify possible sensory experiences in your lessons.

- Use additional sensory supports: objects, pictures, fragrances, music, movements, food, etc.

- Take photographs to record experiences and responses.

- Set up a work/subject buddy rota for the class.

- Identify times when the pupil can work with groups.

MENCAP
Tel: 020 7454 0454, website: www.mencap.org.uk

BEHAVIOURAL, EMOTIONAL AND SOCIAL DEVELOPMENT NEEDS

This term includes 'behavioural, emotional and social difficulties' (BESD) and 'attention deficit disorder' with or without hyperactivity (ADD/ADHD). These difficulties can be seen across the whole ability range and have a continuum of severity. Pupils with special educational needs in this category are those that have persistent difficulties despite an effective school behaviour policy and a personal and social curriculum.

Behavioural, emotional and social difficulties (BESD)

Main characteristics

- inattentive, poor concentration and lacks interest in school/school work

- easily frustrated, anxious about changes

- lacks social skills, unable to work in groups

- unable to work independently, constantly seeking help

- confrontational – verbally aggressive towards other pupils and/or adults

- physically aggressive towards other pupils and/or adults

- destroys their own or others' property

- appears withdrawn, distressed, unhappy, sulky, may self-harm

- lacks confidence, acts extremely frightened, lacks self-esteem

- finds it difficult to communicate

- finds it difficult to accept praise.

How can the science teacher help?

- Check the ability level of the pupil and adapt the level of work to this.

- Consider the pupil's strengths and use them.

- Tell the pupil what you expect in advance, as regards work and behaviour.

- Be particularly aware of safety issues.

- Talk to the pupil to find out a bit about them – try to incorporate their interests in the lesson, e.g. football for forces and motion.

- Set a subject target with a reward system.

- Set up routines for collecting apparatus, etc. Too much freedom of movement around the lab can lead to problems.

- Focus your comments on the behaviour not on the pupil, and offer an alternative way of behaving when correcting the pupil.

- Use positive language and verbal praise whenever possible.

- Tell the pupil what you want them to do: 'I need you to . . .', 'I want you to . . .' rather than ask. This avoids confrontation and the possibility that there is room for negotiation.

- Give the pupil a choice between two options.

- Stick to what you say.

- Be careful when their predictions prove to be wrong – this may precipitate an outburst. Watch out for signs of frustration and step in quickly.

- Involve the pupil in responsibilities to increase self-esteem and confidence.

- Plan a 'time out' system. Ask a colleague for help with this.

SEBDA: The Association of Workers for Children with Emotional and Behavioural Difficulties
Website: www.sebda.org

Attention deficit disorder (with or without hyperactivity) (ADD/ADHD)

'Attention deficit hyperactivity disorder' (ADHD) is a term used to describe children who exhibit over-active behaviour and impulsivity and who have difficulty in paying attention. This is a caused by a form of brain dysfunction of a genetic nature. ADHD can sometimes be controlled effectively by medication. Children of all levels of ability can have ADHD.

Main characteristics

- difficulty in following instructions and completing tasks
- easily distracted by noise, movement of others, objects attracting attention
- often does not listen when spoken to
- fidgets and becomes restless, cannot sit still
- interferes with other pupils' work
- cannot stop talking, interrupts others, calls out
- runs about when inappropriate
- has difficulty in waiting or taking turns
- acts impulsively without thinking about the consequences.

How can the science teacher help?

- Make eye contact and use the pupil's name when speaking to him.
- Keep instructions simple – the one sentence rule.
- Provide clear routines and rules and rehearse them regularly.
- Sit the pupil away from obvious distractions, such as gas taps, windows, the computer.
- Encourage the pupil to repeat back instructions before starting work.
- Give two choices; avoid the option of the pupil saying 'No' by asking 'Do you want to write in blue or black pen?'
- Give advance warning when something is about to happen, change or finish with a time, e.g. 'In two minutes I need you (pupil name) to . . .'.
- Give specific praise – catch him being good, give attention for positive behaviour.
- Give the pupil responsibilities so that others can see him in a positive light and he develops a positive self-image.

ADDISS: The National Attention Deficit Disorder Information and Support Service
Tel: 020 8906 9068, website: www.addiss.co.uk

ADDNET UK
Website: www.btinternet.com/~black.ice/addnet/

COMMUNICATION AND INTERACTION NEEDS

Speech, language and communication difficulties (SLCD)

Pupils with speech, language and communication difficulties (SLCD) have problems with understanding what others say and/or with making others understand what they say. Their development of speech and language skills may be significantly delayed. These difficulties are often resolved during the primary years. Problems that persist beyond the transfer to secondary school will be more severe. Any problem affecting speech, language and communication will have a significant effect on a pupil's self-esteem, and on personal and social relationships. The development of literacy skills is also likely to be affected. Even where pupils learn to decode, they may not understand what they have read. Technological aids, sign language and the use of symbols can give pupils an additional method of communication. Pupils with speech, language and communication difficulties cover the whole range of academic abilities.

Main characteristics

- **Speech difficulties**
  Pupils who have difficulties with expressive language may experience problems in articulation and the production of speech sounds, or in coordinating the muscles that control speech. They may have a stammer or some other form of dysfluency.

- **Language/communication difficulties**
  Pupils with receptive language impairments have difficulty understanding the meaning of what others say. They may use words incorrectly with inappropriate grammatical patterns, have a reduced vocabulary, or find it hard to recall words and express ideas. Some pupils will also have difficulty using and understanding eye contact, facial expression, gesture and body language.

How can the science teacher help?

- Learn the most common signs and symbols for your specific area of science – physical movements can emphasise meaning.

- Use word banks that link pictures and names of apparatus.

- Introduce new vocabulary carefully, with opportunities for pupils to practise saying and writing the words.

- Use labelled diagrams in wall displays and refer to them explicitly.

- Use the pupil's name when addressing them.

- Give one instruction at a time, using short, simple sentences.

- Allow time to respond before repeating a question. Use talking frames to help pupils prepare for feedback sessions.

- Make sure pupils understand what they have to do before starting a task.

- Pair with a work/subject buddy.

- Give access to ICT equipment as appropriate.

- Give written homework instructions.

The ACE centre (Aiding Communication in Education) is a charitable trust providing information, support and training.
Website: www.ace-centre.org.uk

Symbol-supported resources can be easily made with products such as 'Writing with Symbols'.
Website: www.widgit.com

ICAN
Tel: 0845 225 4071, website: www.ican.org.uk

Afasic
Tel: 0845 355 5577 (helpline), 020 7490 9410 (administration)
Email: info@afasic.org.uk, website: www.afasic.org.uk

Autistic spectrum disorders (ASD)

The term 'autistic spectrum disorders' (ASD) is used for a range of disorders affecting the development of social interaction, social communication, and social imagination and flexibility of thought. This is known as the 'triad of impairments'. Pupils with ASD cover the full range of ability and the severity of the impairment varies widely. Some pupils also have learning disabilities or other difficulties. Four times as many boys as girls are diagnosed with an ASD.

Main characteristics

- **Social interaction**
  Pupils with an ASD find it difficult to understand social behaviour and this affects their ability to interact with children and adults. They do not always understand social contexts. They may experience high levels of stress and anxiety in settings that do not meet their needs or when routines are changed. This can lead to inappropriate behaviour.

- **Social communication**
  Understanding and use of non-verbal and verbal communication is impaired. Pupils with an ASD have difficulty understanding the communication of others and in developing effective communication themselves. They have a literal understanding of language. Many are delayed in learning to speak, and some never develop speech at all.

- **Social imagination and flexibility of thought**
  Pupils with an ASD have difficulty in thinking and behaving flexibly which may result in restricted, obsessional or repetitive activities. They are often more interested in objects than people, and have intense interests in such things as trains and vacuum cleaners. Pupils work best when they have a routine. Unexpected changes in those routines will cause distress. Some pupils with autistic spectrum disorders have a different perception of sounds, sights, smell, touch and taste, and this can affect their response to these sensations.

How can science teacher help?

- Provide visual supports in class: objects, pictures, etc.

- Give a symbolic or written order of work for practical investigations.

- Give advance warning of any changes to usual routines.

- Provide a 'safe' area or 'quiet corner' for pupils to work in, if possible (some of the time).

- Avoid using too much eye contact as it can cause distress.

- Give individual instructions using the pupil's name, e.g. 'Paul, bring me your book'.

- Allow access to computers.

- Develop social interactions using a buddy system or circle of friends.

- Avoid using metaphor, idiom or sarcasm – say what you mean in simple language.

- Use special interests to motivate.

Asperger syndrome

Asperger syndrome is a disorder at the able end of the autistic spectrum. People with Asperger syndrome have average to high intelligence but share the same triad of impairments. They often want to make friends but do not understand the complex rules of social interaction. They may have impaired fine and gross motor skills, with writing being a particular problem. Boys are more likely to be affected – with the ratio being 10:1 boys to girls. Because they appear 'odd' and naïve, these pupils are particularly vulnerable to bullying.

Main characteristics

- **Social interaction**
  Pupils with Asperger syndrome want friends but have not developed the strategies necessary for making and sustaining friendships. They find it very difficult to learn social norms and to pick up on social cues. Highly social situations, such as lessons, can cause great anxiety.

- **Social communication**
  Pupils have appropriate spoken language but tend to sound formal and pedantic, using little expression and with an unusual tone of voice. They have difficulty using and understanding non-verbal language such as facial expression, gesture, body language and eye contact. They have a literal understanding of language and do not grasp implied meanings.

- **Social imagination**
  Pupils with Asperger syndrome need structured environments, and to have routines they understand and can anticipate. They excel at learning facts and figures, but have difficulty understanding abstract concepts and in generalising information and skills. They often have all-consuming special interests.

How can the science teacher help?

- Create as calm a classroom environment as possible.

- Allow the pupil to sit in the same place for each lesson (a quiet area can be helpful for some pupils).

- Set up a work buddy system for your lessons.

- Provide additional visual cues in class.

- Allow time to process questions and respond.

- Make sure pupils understand what to do.

- Allow alternatives to writing for recording.

- Use visual timetables and task activity lists.

- Prepare for changes to routines well in advance.

- Give written homework instructions and stick into an exercise book.

- Have your own class rules and apply them consistently.

The National Autistic Society
Tel: 0845 070 4004 (helpline), 020 7833 2299
Email: nas@nas.org.uk, website: www.nas.org.uk

Semantic pragmatic disorder (SPD)

Semantic pragmatic disorder (SPD) is a communication disorder which falls within the autistic spectrum. Semantic refers to the meanings of words and phrases and pragmatic refers to the use of language in a social context. Pupils with this disorder have difficulties understanding the meaning of what people say and in using language to communicate effectively.

Pupils with SPD find it difficult to extract the central meaning – saliency – of situations.

Main characteristics

- delayed language development
- fluent speech but may sound stilted or over-formal
- may repeat phrases out of context from videos or adult conversations
- difficulty understanding abstract concepts
- limited or inappropriate use of eye contact, facial expression or gesture
- motor skills problems

How can the science teacher help?

- Sit the pupil at front of the room to avoid distractions.
- Use visual supports: objects, pictures, symbols, etc.
- Pair with a work/subject buddy.
- Create a calm working environment with clear classroom rules.
- Be specific and unambiguous when giving instructions.
- Make sure instructions are understood, especially when using subject-specific vocabulary that can have another meaning in a different context.

Afasic
Tel: 0845 355 5577 (helpline), 020 7490 9410 (administration)
Email: info@afasic.org.uk, website: www.afasic.org.uk

SENSORY AND/OR PHYSICAL NEEDS

Hearing impairment (HI)

The term 'hearing impairment' is a generic term used to describe all hearing loss. The main types of loss are monaural, conductive, sensory and mixed loss. The degree of hearing loss is described as mild, moderate, severe or profound.

How can the science teacher help?

- Check the degree of loss the pupil has.

- Check the best seating position (e.g. away from the hum of OHP and computers, with good ear to speaker).

- Check that the pupil can see your face for facial expressions and lip reading.

- Provide a list of vocabulary, context and visual cues, especially for new subjects.

- During class discussion allow only one pupil to speak at a time and indicate where the speaker is.

- Check that any aids are working and whether there is any other specialist equipment available.

- Be sensitive when teaching topics such as sound.

The Royal National Institute for Deaf People (RNID)
Tel: 0808 808 0123 (information line), website: www.rnid.org.uk

British Deaf Association (BDA)
Tel: 0870 770 3300 (helpline), website: www.signcommunity.org.uk

The British Association of Teachers of the Deaf (BATOD)
Website: www.batod.org.uk

Visual impairment (VI)

'Visual impairment' refers to a range of difficulties including those pupils with monocular vision (vision in one eye), those who are partially sighted and those who are blind. Pupils with visual impairment cover the whole ability range and some pupils may have other SEN.

How can the science teacher help?

- Check the optimum position for the pupil, e.g. for a monocular pupil their good eye should be towards the action.

- Always provide the pupil with his own copy of the text.

- Provide enlarged print copies of written text.

- Check use of ICT (enlarged icons, talking text, teach keyboard skills).

- Do not stand with your back to the window as this creates a silhouette and makes it harder for the pupil to see you.

- Draw the pupil's attention to displays – which they may not notice.

- Make sure the floor is kept free of clutter.

- Tell the pupil if there is a change to the layout of a space.

- Ask if there is any specialist equipment available (enlarged print dictionaries, lights, talking scales, thermometers).

- Be sensitive when teaching topics such as light.

- Extra safety measures may need to be put in place and preparations made in good time.

- Research the availability of low-vision aids such as microscope cameras and magnifier units (the LA Sensory Support Service may help).

Royal National Institute for the Blind (RNIB)
Tel: 020 7388 1266, website: www.rnib.org.uk

Multi-sensory impairment

Pupils with multi-sensory impairment have a combination of visual and hearing difficulties. They may also have additional disabilities that make their situation complex. A pupil with these difficulties is likely to have a high level of individual support.

How can the science teacher help?

- Liaise with support staff to ascertain the appropriate provision within science lessons.

- Consideration will need to be given to alternative means of communication.

- Be prepared to be flexible and to adapt tasks, targets and assessment procedures.

Cerebral palsy (CP)

Cerebral palsy (CP) is a persistent disorder of movement and posture. It is caused by damage or lack of development to part of the brain before or during birth or in early childhood. Problems vary from slight clumsiness to more severe lack of control of movements. Pupils with CP may also have learning difficulties. They may use a wheelchair or other mobility aid.

Main characteristics

There are three main forms of cerebral palsy:

- *spasticity* – disordered control of movement associated with stiffened muscles

- *athetosis* – frequent involuntary movements

- *ataxia* – an unsteady gait with balance difficulties and poor spatial awareness.

Pupils may also have communication difficulties.

How can the science teacher help?

- Talk to parents, the physiotherapist – and the pupil.

- Consider the classroom layout.

- Have high academic expectations.

- Use visual supports: objects, pictures, symbols, etc.

- Arrange a work/subject buddy.

- Speak directly to the pupil rather than through a teaching assistant.

- Ensure access to appropriate IT equipment – and that it is used.

Scope
Tel: 0808 800 3333 (helpline), 020 7619 7100 (general)
Email: cphelpline@scope.org.uk, website: www.scope.org.uk

Physical disability (PD)

There is a wide range of physical disabilities (PD), and pupils with PD cover all academic abilities. Some pupils are able to access the curriculum and learn effectively without additional educational provision – they have a disability but do not have a special educational need. For other pupils, the impact on their education may be severe, and the school will need to make adjustments to enable them to access the curriculum.

Some pupils with a physical disability have associated medical conditions which may impact on their mobility. These include cerebral palsy, heart disease, spina bifida and hydrocephalus, and muscular dystrophy. Pupils with physical disabilities may also have sensory impairments, neurological problems or learning difficulties. They may use a wheelchair and/or additional mobility aids. Some pupils will be mobile but may have significant fine motor difficulties which require support. Others may need augmentative or alternative communication aids.

Pupils with a physical disability may need to miss lessons to attend physiotherapy or medical appointments. They are also likely to become very tired as they expend greater effort to complete everyday tasks. Schools will need to be flexible and sensitive to individual pupil needs.

How can the science teacher help?

- Get to know pupils and parents and they will help you make the right adjustments.

- Maintain high expectations.

- Consider the classroom layout – is there enough space for wheelchairs and/or walking frames?

- Equipment should be at an accessible height; adjustable tables are useful.

- Allow the pupil to leave lessons a few minutes early to avoid busy corridors and give time to get to the next lesson.

- Set homework earlier in the lesson so instructions are not missed.

- Speak directly to the pupil rather than through a teaching assistant.

- Let pupils make their own decisions.

- Ensure access to appropriate IT equipment for the lesson – and that it is used.

- Allow alternative ways of recording work.

- Plan to cover work missed through medical or physiotherapy appointments.

- Be sensitive to fatigue, especially at the end of the school day.

- Be prepared to adapt apparatus to allow pupil to access practical work.

ICT adaptations are available from companies such as SEMERC (www.semerc.com) and Inclusive Technology (www.inclusive.co.uk).

Tourette syndrome

Tourette syndrome is a neurological disorder characterised by tics. Tics are involuntary rapid or sudden movements or sounds that are frequently repeated. There is a wide range of severity of the condition with some people having no need to seek medical help whilst others have a socially disabling condition. The tics can be suppressed for a short time but will be more noticeable when the pupil is anxious or excited.

Main characteristics

- **Physical tics**
  Range from simple blinking or nodding through more complex movements to more extreme conditions such as echopraxia (imitating actions seen) or copropraxia (repeatedly making obscene gestures).

- **Vocal tics**
  Vocal tics may be as simple as throat clearing or coughing but can progress to be as extreme as echolalia (the repetition of what was last heard) or coprolalia (the repetition of obscene words).

Tourette syndrome itself causes no behavioural or educational problems but other, associated disorders such as attention deficit hyperactivity disorder (ADHD) or obsessive-compulsive disorder (OCD) may be present.

How can the science teacher help?

- Establish a rapport with the pupil.

- Talk to the parents.

- Agree an 'escape route' signal should the tics become disruptive.

- Allow the pupil to sit at the back of the room to prevent staring.

- Give access to a computer to reduce the need for handwriting.

- Make sure pupil is not teased or bullied.

- Help other pupils to understand and accept the condition.

- Be alert for signs of anxiety or depression.

Tourette Syndrome (UK) Association
Tel: 0845 458 1252 (helpline), 01383 629 600 (administration)
Email: enquiries@tsa.org.uk, website: www.tsa.org.uk

An Inclusive Learning Environment

Science is all about discovery. The greatest of the discoveries have been made where scientists observe particular phenomena, generate ideas to explain these and then search for further evidence to either prove or disprove these ideas. As part of this evidence-gathering process a scientist needs to employ a range of practical skills which include making observations that involve the use of all of the senses. It is our job, as teachers, to develop all of these skills in our students.

Students with special educational needs might find various parts of this discovery process more challenging than other students. In this chapter we will consider how we can minimise any barriers that might make the subject inaccessible to students. Our objective in this is to create a supportive environment which will maximise learning opportunities, make lessons more efficient and allow the students to focus on scientific learning.

The physical environment

Scientific laboratories are not always the most student-friendly environments and, whilst the philosophy and practice of the teaching of science has changed over the last few years, many of the rooms in which it is taught have changed very little. Ask most parents what a school science laboratory is like and they will remember benches, high stools, even the smell of the laboratory. In many schools, very little has changed.

A great deal of time is spent in preparation of lessons and marking students' work, but the actual layout of the room is often not given the priority it deserves. Even the colour of the walls can have an influence on the students. Most science teachers have little control over the positioning of things such as gas taps and the type of furniture in the laboratory but, where opportunities arise, planning the layout of furniture and equipment carefully can have a great influence on the performance of students. The creation of discrete features such as quiet areas can only enhance scientific learning. Never be afraid to change things around, and if it does not work, change it again. Difficulties can arise when teachers do not have the luxury of their own laboratory but have to share; discussion between colleagues is essential, especially when trying to improve the learning environment for students with SEN.

Considerations

- The furniture and how it is arranged to allow access to all areas and services, and to allow the students to work in appropriate pairs and groups.

- The use of colour and wall displays.

- Equipment and its placement and labelling.

Furniture should be arranged, wherever possible, to allow access for all students, including those in wheelchairs or with walking aids. (Pupils with visual impairment (VI) will benefit from the room layout remaining constant, but will cope with furniture being moved around if this is pointed out to them.)

Benches may be static, but seating can usually be moved around and allow for pupils being able to see the board, a demonstration or a projection screen. Is the room flexible enough to allow students the opportunity of grouping together for any discussion work? All these are important points.

Consider the amount of furniture in the room. Is there too much? Tidy storage of coats and bags is an important point of safety in all situations, but for pupils with visual impairment and mobility difficulties it is even more so.

Do any of the students require benches that are height-adjusting to accommodate wheelchairs? This furniture may not be permanently required, but discussion is needed with the special needs department within the school to see what provision can be made for the duration of the time certain students spend in the laboratory. There are a number of specialist suppliers of such furniture, such as adjustable desks to cater for the different heights of wheelchairs, and adjustable-height chairs for students with posture difficulties. If a student feels comfortable in the laboratory, they are more likely to engage in the lesson.

Specialist equipment for pupils with VI can often be borrowed from the LA Sensory Support Service. Sloping desktops, magnifiers and specially adapted science equipment such as scales and thermometers with large-format gradations are often useful for other pupils too.

Walls and displays

If we are to avoid sensory overload (which can be an issue with pupils on the ASD spectrum especially), but want to create the best learning environment for our students, the colours used in the laboratory are important. The colour of the walls is often out of the hands of the teacher, but improvements can be achieved with backing paper, posters and students' work. Colours do seem to affect people: most pastel colours are calming, especially pale greens; dark blue is depressing; red provokes anger and yellow is seen as uplifting.

It is important to plan how to organise wall coverings and have some areas that are changed frequently, especially if things such as key words and objectives are displayed. Wall covering may include:

- students' work

- objectives

- key words (and meanings)

- posters related to units being covered

- science posters, e.g. on safety

- spelling of common scientific words

- pieces of equipment to illustrate work or stimulate interest.

Care is needed not to make walls so busy that they become a distraction for pupils. Give careful consideration to the placement of displays and label clearly so that they can be seen from a distance and have meaning for the students. Place at a suitable height – if the teacher is over 6 ft tall, he will have a very different view of things to a Year 7 pupil who is 4 ft 6 in, or a Year 9 student seated in a wheelchair.

It is important to select a range of student work to display on the walls, to celebrate their successes and achievements. It would be all too easy just to display the neatest and most colourful work, which is often just representative of a few of the students in the class. This can also favour girls; why not have a count of the number of boys and number of girls represented in the displays in your lab and see if there is a balance? Every student needs to have their successes celebrated. Displayed work can be much more meaningful with a comment from the teacher to say why that particular piece has won a place in the display. Most schools have a digital camera, and displaying photographs of pupils engaged in practical work can overcome the situation where some pupils never produce the sort of work which looks good on the wall.

It is important to share the objectives and outcomes of the lesson with the students, and this is discussed further in Chapter 5. It is good practice to display these objectives and outcomes throughout the lesson so that the students can refer to them to help target their work.

Key word lists can be valuable for helping students to use the correct scientific terminology and the correct spellings. Static displays of key words soon become 'wallpaper', however, which pupils no longer notice. These words need to be changed regularly and explained as they go up on the wall. The words become more meaningful if they are supported with definitions and if they are used in the lessons. These can be made into games, quizzes and quick revision.

Owing to the number of groups a science teacher may have in the classroom each day, consideration needs to be paid to where these are displayed and they need to be large enough for students to see. It may also be important to colour-code them for each group or year. It may be useful to use pictures, diagrams or symbols with key words; this is especially helpful to pupils with learning difficulties.

Certain colour combinations of words and backgrounds can be difficult to read for some students. As a general rule of thumb, if the words are to be read close up, then a dark colour on a pale background is best; however, if the displays are to be read from a distance, then pale colours (such as yellow or white) on dark backgrounds (such as dark blue) are often easier to read. You do, however, need to consider students with colour blindness and some colour combinations can be easier for students with dyslexia; the best solution is to ask the students which colour combinations they find easiest to read. This could even be the subject of an investigation.

Equipment within the laboratory

Apparatus needs to be clearly labelled and placed in accessible areas. It may be appropriate and time saving to prepare apparatus before the start of a practical lesson. This will help those pupils who have poor organisational skills and allow them to actually get on with the investigation. It is good practice to group apparatus together, for example have heating apparatus, such as Bunsen burners, bench mats, tripods and gauzes, within the same area; this cuts down unnecessary movement.

For those students who experience motor skills difficulties, consider having adapted apparatus available. There are a number of suppliers of adapted apparatus, such as Nottingham Rehab (see Resources p.119 for contact details). Alternatively, you can consider adapting standard apparatus to meet the needs of your students. For example, many students with poor motor skills find it difficult to use a Bunsen burner. You can solder a piece of metal, to act as a lever, which enables these students to move the collar round without having to use the thumb and first finger. The type of flame can now be altered with just a knuckle. (Make sure that equipment is well-maintained to ensure smooth working.)

When adapting apparatus, it is essential to think about safety. Check with CLEAPPS and also with the health and safety officer in your school or for your county to ensure the apparatus would be considered safe. Adapted apparatus could include:

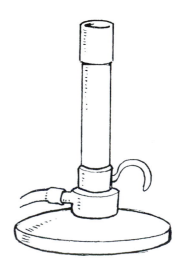

- gauze laced to the top of the tripod to stop it being accidentally knocked off

- plastic measuring jugs instead of measuring cylinders if approximate amounts are required

- a small funnel when there is no option but to use a measuring cylinder

- foam collars round the measuring cylinder to enable a better grip

- for sensory-impaired students, a moisture sensor connected to a buzzer to buzz (or a light to light) when a container is full

- rims of glassware painted in black to make it easier for some visually impaired students to see

- a foam collar round a thermometer to allow easier grip

- pieces of non-slip material on which to stand apparatus

- very shallow trays that pupils can put apparatus in so that if substances are spilt they are contained

- protective aprons/lab coats

- book rests

- a free-standing magnifying glass. Students with visual impairments might find reading scales difficult, particularly on things such as thermometers that have small scales. For these students you can use talking thermometers and instruments with tactile scales.

This equipment could be stored with the other items or put into trays forming sets of apparatus. It is good practice to have a few sets available; this enables all those students who feel in need of extra support to appreciate the value of the apparatus and it does not make the student with a particular difficulty feel different from the rest of a group and so aids their self-esteem. When demonstrating experiments use the adapted apparatus sometimes.

Other adaptations that may be useful include:

- using retort stands for beakers and test tubes so that students can support apparatus; this is useful for students with limited motor skills. If the jaws of the clamp are not closed fully, they can slide the apparatus in or out easily.

- putting foam around the handles of test tube holders and crucible tongs to increase the grip for those with poor motor skills.

- putting a little Vaseline onto beakers to see when they are warm. Students will be able to see it melt (chocolate can also be used but can be a little messy).

- for stirring, use a magnetic stirrer; these can reduce spills, which is particularly important when using harmful chemicals.

Practical work can be rewarding for students with sensory or motor difficulties if the equipment is carefully considered and adaptations made when necessary. The important thing is to consider the problems the students are having and come up with a piece of apparatus to suit their requirements, allowing them access to the curriculum and increasing their self-esteem. If there is a teaching assistant who knows the pupils well, use their invaluable insights into the needs of individuals and ask their advice about pre-empting problems.

(Teachers may have problems appreciating the difficulties experienced by some pupils. Appendix 4.2 contains some ideas that could be used during a faculty meeting for SEN training. Tasks such as fastening buttons whilst wearing thick gardening gloves, with someone asking you questions at the same time, demonstrate how the physical act detracts from the content of the work.)

Clear labelling of apparatus and substances is essential. It is possible to buy labelling machines that type in Braille; the dual labelling of trays can be useful for those students with visual difficulties. Colours and symbols will help some students, so try using a system of colour-coding and diagrams when labelling apparatus. It is worth making a room plan of where key apparatus is stored and displaying this on the wall to help those students likely to forget. You could also give a plan to anyone assisting in the laboratory.

The communicating classroom

Communication can take many forms, with written and spoken language being the most obviously recognisable ones. However, the way we speak, our body language or even what is not said can be equally important. There are many skills involved in being an effective communicator. As teachers we need to develop and practise these skills but also teach them to pupils. Other adults who interact with students, such as teaching assistants and laboratory technicians, also need to be aware of the importance of good communication and act as good role models.

It is vital that teachers speak clearly and unambiguously to students, using scientific terminology relevant to the age and ability of the various students in the group. This may sound like common sense, but the language and tone has an important role to play in allowing students to access the curriculum. Be prepared to repeat key concepts or instructions and, if students ask what seem to be obvious questions, try to answer with patience, keeping the tone of your voice even rather than giving the impression that you are frustrated at having to repeat things for them. It may also be important to have a copy of key points, objectives and instructions on the board.

Clear explanations of terminology can prevent a lot of misunderstanding and failure (some possibilities for confusion are listed below). Remember that for pupils with learning difficulties, especially those with hearing impairments and those with disorders on the autistic spectrum, the use of metaphor can be misleading (an explosion of colour, killer explosion).

WORDS WITH MORE THAN ONE MEANING:

- solution
- resistance
- concentration
- light
- rays/raise.

Questioning skills

Questioning is a key skill for any teacher. We do not just ask questions to test if the students understand a certain concept; we want to help them develop their ideas. By verbalising an idea, it helps this idea to become more secure. This is therefore even more important for some students with special educational needs. Verbal reasoning provides a vehicle for these students to express their ideas without the burden of having to write. When written accounts are required, skilful questioning can prepare pupils for the writing task and help them to organise their thoughts.

Questions can vary greatly in their level of conceptual difficulty, and there are different ways of categorising these: perhaps the most used of these is called Bloom's Taxonomy (Bloom, 1976). Bloom's Taxonomy and how it can be related to questions is shown in the table below.

BLOOM'S TAXONOMY

Classification	Definition	Active words
KNOWLEDGE	Knowing facts and describing what is observed.	Define, state, list, name, write, recall, recognise, identify.
COMPREHENSION	Using ideas in familiar contexts, explaining how and why something happens.	Summarise, explain, interpret, classify, convert, illustrate, translate.
APPLICATION	Using ideas, knowledge, understanding in a new context.	Use, solve, apply, modify, relate, predict.
ANALYSIS	Breaking information down, seeking patterns.	Deduce, contrast, distinguish, arrange, deconstruct, discuss, devise, plan, criticise, separate, break down.
SYNTHESIS	Generalising from given information, linking ideas and theories to make explanations or predictions.	Restate, organise, generalise, derive, discuss, formulate.
EVALUATION	Comparing and discriminating between ideas, making choices based on reasoned argument, verifying the value of evidence.	Summarise, judge, appraise, defend, argue, validate, compare, contrast, assess, verify.

The first category, 'knowledge', is what is often described as 'closed' questioning: this is where there is normally only one answer which is correct. This type of question does not challenge the students to think and expand their ideas. It can also be disheartening to some students, who find it difficult to recall facts and ideas, to always get the answer to this type of question wrong.

As you progress through Bloom's Taxonomy, the conceptual demand, and therefore the level of challenge of the question, increases. Questions need to be directed towards individual students so that they are at the appropriate level to provide just enough challenge to extend the student. It is therefore important to prepare the key questions, around which the lesson is based, before the lesson starts.

'Big Questions' are those for which you would not expect there to be an immediate response: the students need to think about them and develop their ideas. It is often more appropriate for students to work in groups to share and develop their ideas for these Big Questions. The level of demand of the question can be changed by changing the way the question is phrased.

For example, the initial question might be: 'Name the seven life processes' – this question would be categorised as a 'knowledge' question and the students would be able to get the answer completely right, partially right or wrong. This could be changed into a series of questions that ask the students to apply their ideas in science to different situations for example: 'If all living things go to the toilet (excrete), how does a tree do this?' – this question would be categorised as a 'synthesis' question. It has a higher conceptual demand and is designed to get the students to think. Students may experience more success with this type of question, because they are not simply being asked to recall; the ideas behind excretion are also more likely to become embedded as a result.

When asking any question you need to consider 'wait time': this is the time between when you finish asking the question and when you jump in because no one has answered it. Research suggests that the average 'wait time' can be less than one second; this is too short a time for any student and especially so for many with SEN. It is therefore important to provide sufficient 'wait time'. The length of 'wait time' also depends on the type of question. A simple 'knowledge' question might need a 'wait time' of a few seconds. However, a synthesis question, especially if it is being discussed in groups, might need several minutes.

To help the students understand what is expected of them, it is useful to signal the amount of time they have to answer the question. You could always start with, 'this is a four-second question . . .'. It is also possible to buy large hourglass-style egg timers, which can range from about 30 seconds to about 15 minutes in time capacity. So, when you ask your Big Question, why not let the students know that it is a five-minute question to be discussed in groups and turn the hourglass over to let them know their time has started.

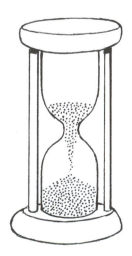

An alternative approach to 'wait time' is for the teacher to judge 'time up' by reference to a particular student who has proved herself to be conscientious and tends to finish work (thinking or writing) in reasonable time

When asking questions of the whole class, if you allow the students to put their hands up to signal that they wish to answer the question, this will always encourage the same students to attempt to answer. Often, it is the students with special educational needs who misses out. The alternative is to develop a culture where the students do not expect to put their hands up; questions are therefore directed at individuals. This encourages all students to get involved. There is often an expectation that if the student is asked a question then they should attempt to answer it. This has an implication on the type of question you might ask of individual students. It might be inappropriate to ask a certain student to name the male parts of a plant, because you know that they have difficulty with recall-type questions. However, the same student might be asked to describe how they think a bee might collect pollen from a plant and through their answer to this question you might encourage them to use the names for the parts accurately.

Allowing students to ask questions is also a valuable form of communication. To develop confidence, allowing students to write down their question and read it out is useful. Having a question box and allowing students to write their own questions to put in can be a valuable activity and can be used as a valuable plenary session.

Working in groups

Speaking within a whole-group setting can be daunting for many students and therefore working with a partner or within a small group can be valuable in developing their self-confidence. Similarly, reading aloud is very difficult for some pupils and the chance to rehearse beforehand will result in a more successful outcome.

Within the laboratory, paired group work is often used for practical sessions. At such times it is vital to ensure both students contribute to the actual work, even if the less confident one allows their partner or support assistant to take the lead role. However, as the class teacher it is important that you do not allow one of the students to 'hide behind' the other. It is easy to assume that students and support staff automatically know how to 'support' without taking over, but this is often not the case. A role-play activity demonstrating how to, and how not to, support learners and learning can be useful and make a significant and immediate impact.

Breaking the work down into small packages is important, especially in a practical session. Within the group there may be students with short attention spans and unless the task is presented in small packages they may fail to complete the work successfully. This is also important for those students with literacy problems: if they are faced with a whole lesson of written work, they will find concentration a problem and may not complete the work or may become disruptive. Minimising the amount of writing required (and drawing of apparatus) allows more time to concentrate on doing and thinking about the science behind the practical work. There is rarely a need for students to produce a formal 'write-up' of the experiment, as it is the findings which are important. Ready-prepared record sheets can do a lot to speed up the process of recording and make it more accurate (see Appendices 4.3 and 4.4).

different amounts. Time can also be an issue for many pupils with special needs. Visual prompts for these aspects of work in science can be very valuable – either up on the wall or clipped into books/folders or as plastic-covered 'crib-sheets' on the benches. (See Appendices 4.7–4.17, and the accompanying CD for samples.)

ICT

ICT is vital for an inclusive laboratory. It can enhance the work of both the student and the teacher. Students can report back via a PowerPoint presentation, or use a worksheet which could be copied and handed out or projected onto the board. This enables those students with a range of special needs to participate to a fuller extent as the written word can be redrafted, spell-checked and presented in an easily readable way.

ICT also provides a valuable tool for teachers, allowing you to store any resources produced electronically and then adapt this to suit the needs of individual students in a number of ways. You can alter the size of print, simplify language, make work more accessible through the use of DART (Directed Activity Related to Text; see Chapter 5) or draw tables for students to complete with data from observations.

By using digital video cameras and webcams, experiments can be recorded so students have the opportunity to watch them again during the lesson if they do not fully understand a practical procedure. For some students, viewing a video clip of, for example, using a measuring cylinder correctly can be very useful.

Instructions for performing investigations and experiments are often an issue in science lessons. If you just give verbal instruction, there will always be a group of students who have not managed to follow all of the steps. If you give written instructions, the readability of technical directions might cause problems for some students. If you do both, you could still run the risk of not reaching all students. One possible answer to this is to use a digital camera to take photographs of someone performing the experiment, then present these as a sequence of steps within a PowerPoint presentation. By all means add instructions and, when these refer to a piece of apparatus, you can draw an arrow onto the relevant item to illustrate this. It is possible for this type of presentation to keep restarting on a cycle and move on automatically, which would allow the students to work at their own pace and look up to find the correct stage.

Science is an ideal subject for the development of motor skills, but if the practical work is not essential for the learning objectives, then by allowing students to use computer simulations it enables them to access the scientific concepts. Computer simulations can also be used to reinforce concepts. For example, when studying radioactivity at key stage 4, the absorption of the different types of radiation can be demonstrated, and the students can then perform their own virtual experiments using a simulation.

With datalogging equipment, students do not have to record individual readings for an experiment and then plot a graph from each of these points. The computer software does this for them and they can concentrate on developing scientific explanations for the shape of the graph. For students with motor skill problems, this enhances their progress as they have to spend little time on manipulating apparatus or graph paper. Students do need practice in drawing graphs, but it is important to consider the purpose of the graph in the context of the work.

By combining datalogging equipment with a dataprojector, it is possible to demonstrate learning points without the students performing practical work. This would not necessarily be the preferred teaching method every lesson, but there might be occasions where it is appropriate. For example, you might want to set up a cooling curve experiment using octadecanoic acid. This could run whilst the students are engaged in a different learning activity. The teacher could use the projected results from this to discuss melting points.

For readers who do not have a dataprojector (and little chance of getting one in the near future), there are cheaper alternatives. For example, a 'scan converter' connects to the VGA port on your computer and will convert the signal to PAL, which can be then viewed on a television. Whilst an image from a dataprojector to a big screen would be both bigger and sharper, this might be better than nothing and help some students. Do not forget the use of digital microscopes, which can be really useful for students who through either visual impairment or poor motor skills find it difficult to use a conventional microscope. The main limitation of these, however, is that the resolution is nowhere near as good.

For some students the use of Clicker software is a valuable tool. By entering words for a particular topic (this could be done by the teaching assistant), the students will be able to concentrate on the scientific concepts rather than the words. Clicker can be used to support students' writing at several levels, and there are three examples in Appendix 4.18 to illustrate this. The first example shows how pictures can be used to support the students' writing at the most basic level. The second example shows how a complete word list can be used so that the students can write entirely by clicking on the appropriate words. The third example shows how the key scientific vocabulary can be provided with the students typing in the rest of the paragraph. Clicker is published by Crick Software (www.cricksoft.com).

Also available from Crick Software is ClozePro. This is a piece of software which can be used to produce cloze procedures, and there is more detail about these in the next chapter. These can be either developed for the students to use on the computer or printed out as worksheets. Text can be scanned in to produce activities fairly rapidly, again a possible task for the teaching assistant. Examples of the use of ClozePro are shown in Appendix 4.19. The first example shows how a cloze exercise can be produced with a word list of choices. The second shows how a drop-down list can be produced for each blank. The third example shows a spelling exercise.

There is a range of modified equipment for pupils with special needs: large-key keyboards, touchscreens, switch access devices. For further information and catalogues, see the Bibliography and the Resources and Useful Websites sections. Organisations such as Becta (www.becta.org.uk) and ACE (www. ace-centre.org.uk) are also on hand to offer advice and guidance.

The CD-ROM produced by the Association for Science Education and NASEN entitled *Inclusive Science and Special Educational Needs* has some useful materials for students with special educational needs (see www.issen.org. uk/cd.htm). This resource is divided into five main sections:

- investigations and projects
- focus activities
- words, symbols and pictures
- SEN in the science department
- further resources and ideas.

The CD-ROM makes good use of sound, so the use of headphones could be valuable to avoid distractions.

Conclusion

Developing an inclusive laboratory is not attained without hard work. It is important to have a good knowledge of the strengths and weaknesses of the students, use the support that may be provided wisely, and build on your own skills. If one thing fails, do not give up but evaluate where things went wrong in order to develop the approach for the next time.

It is important to consider the following when developing an inclusive laboratory:

- Do not make the laboratory an overloaded sensory environment.
- Have well-placed and clearly labelled equipment.
- Place furniture carefully.
- Make good use of wall colour and displays.
- Be clear about asking questions.
- Use a range of strategies to develop communication skills.
- Use small-staged practical work to develop practical skills.
- Use small groups and partners to develop oral skills.
- Link with the mathematics faculty to check out how mathematical concepts are taught.
- Use ICT to allow students to access the curriculum more by developing information gathering and recording of ideas.

Science should be sensory, interactive, stimulating and fun everyone. With understanding and forward planning, science teachers can create an inclusive environment that caters for all pupils.

CHAPTER 5

Teaching and Learning

It is the last lesson of the day, the Year 7 group coming into the laboratory have just had PE and some of them are late. You want them to design and carry out an investigation into which natural materials would make the most suitable indicator. The laboratory is hot, even with the windows open, and there are only five mortar and pestles available for the whole class. After 15 minutes of interruptions you realise they are unsure about what you want them to do: those who arrived first are bored of hearing the same instructions for the fifth time. By the end of the lesson fewer than half of the class have successfully made and tested their indicator. To compound the issue, you then spend the half hour immediately after the lesson cleaning red cabbage and beetroot out of the sinks.

Some aspects of this situation are out of the hands of the science teacher – the time of day, the weather and the lesson immediately prior to yours are definitely out of your control. However, there are things that you can change which will increase the chances of your lesson having a successful outcome. Communication with colleagues where students consistently arrive late is important, planning and ordering apparatus in advance to avoid clashes can help, and thinking of alternative methods of presenting the instructions can prove to be useful. Thinking about how the students can pack away their apparatus can pay dividends: a bucket for certain waste materials, appointing monitors to oversee certain aspects of the clearing away and establishing routes can all help.

Being flexible enough to change the task when you realise things are going badly wrong is an important skill to develop. As a teacher you need to develop activities which will lead to effective learning. Kyriacou writes on this subject:

> The essence of effective teaching lies in the ability of the teacher to set up a learning experience which brings about the desired educational outcomes. For this to take place, each pupil must be engaged in the activity of learning.
>
> (Kyriacou 1997:21)

Although this statement is generic to all teaching, it is especially important to consider the links between learning – and the teaching which facilitates this – when planning work for students with SEN. Many of the ideas presented in this chapter apply to all science lessons with groups of all abilities but are particularly pertinent when considering classes with students with SEN.

The way a lesson is structured can have a big effect on the outcome. We are not looking for a formulaic approach to teaching where every lesson has the same structure come what may. What this chapter hopes to achieve is to share a series of possible issues to consider when planning the lesson. These are tried and tested ways of motivating the students whatever their attainment – some of these techniques might even work for the last lesson on a Friday immediately after PE!

This chapter is ordered around a possible lesson structure, and this structure consists of:

- an entry activity

- sharing of objectives and learning outcomes

- an engagement activity or starter

- the main part of the lesson

- a plenary.

This is an extension of the much-talked-about 'three-part lesson'. We will, however, try to avoid describing it as a 'five-part lesson' – it is not a structure which would apply to every circumstance; it is meant to be flexible. There are many issues to be considered in the 'main' part of the lesson, so when considering this we will need to break this part of the chapter down into different parts.

Entry activities

There are many reasons why the members of a class might arrive in dribs and drabs, not least because they have just had PE and take differing amounts of time to get dressed. For some students, particularly those with BESD or with ADHD, the last thing you want is to give them time with no meaningful task, just sitting waiting for the last one to arrive. For all students, lesson time is valuable and the sooner you can engage the students with learning activities the more productive the lesson will be.

Entry activities can come in many forms but the main uniting factor is that they engage the students in a task that they can undertake immediately on entry without the need for lengthy instructions from the teacher. This could be a valuable time for students to respond to feedback from their homework. Often in marking books you will make comments that the students should respond to, for example: 'Add arrows to this diagram to show the effect of friction', or 'Use the idea of particles moving faster when they are hotter to explain why the sugar dissolves faster in the hotter water'. These are formative comments that the students could respond to immediately on entering the room and collecting their books.

This could also be an opportunity for the students to engage with an activity which links back to the previous lesson. A wordsearch or anagram exercise to revise the key vocabulary thus far in the unit can help some students make important links. An activity where the students draw or label a diagram to show an element of their learning from the previous lesson could also provide valuable insights into how well the outcomes from the previous lesson have been embedded. Examples of these types of entry activity can be found on the accompanying CD.

Learning objectives and learning outcomes

It is all too easy to teach our favourite lessons, particularly practicals, without considering how well these match the learning objectives. For example, is an experiment where the students scrape the inside of their mouth to make a slide of cheek cells really the best way of teaching about the structure of animal cells? Most of the students are not looking at animal cells but rather a bit of their breakfast anyway! This can lead to big misconceptions.

By considering the lesson objective carefully, it is easier to match the learning activities to this objective and it is easier to differentiate outcomes so that every student has a chance of success. The starting point for developing the objective is often some form of published curriculum; this could be the National Curriculum, the Framework for Teaching Science, QCA Schemes of Work or an examination syllabus. The first statement in the Framework for Teaching Science for the Year 7 Yearly Teaching Objectives for Cells reads: 'Describe a simple model for cells that recognises those features all cells have in common and the differences between animal and plant cells.' This contains too much content for most students to cover in one lesson and it is not written in language which is easy for many to understand. This needs to be written into a suitable lesson objective, such as: 'Describe the structure of an animal cell'. You might want to make this even more child-friendly by introducing a character to share the objectives with the students. This character is 'WALT', which stands for 'We Are Learning To . . .'.

WALT could take many forms, from a face on a poster or interactive whiteboard slide to a glove puppet. The objective then becomes: 'We Are Learning To describe the structure of an animal cell.'

This does not, however, tell the students what they have to do to be successful – this is where we need to use learning outcomes.

The learning outcomes for the lesson tell the students what they have to do to be successful. This is where you can introduce differentiation, so that there are outcomes at different levels. The QCA Schemes of Work use three levels of outcomes which they describe as:

- Some pupils will not have made so much progress and will . . .
- Most pupils will . . .
- Some pupils will have progressed further and will . . .

This is rather long and difficult to understand for some students. Simpler mechanisms that are easier to use are:

- All, Most and Some

or

- Must, Should and Could.

You might want to introduce another character, called 'WILF', which stands for 'What I am Looking For . . .'. So, the learning outcomes for the lesson on animal cells might be: 'What I'm Looking For is that . . .

- **All** of you label a diagram to show the different parts of an animal cell.
- **Most** of you describe the function of each of these parts.
- **Some** of you explain why the cell membrane is not completely watertight.'

These outcomes are in order of cognitive demand. Labelling is something achievable to all students; some students will be able to draw their own diagram and label it whilst some SEN students might need the further support of a prepared diagram and labels. Describing is then a higher-order outcome, which most students in Year 7 should be able to do. Explaining why represents the highest level of demand for this lesson, and this might be an extension activity aimed at the higher attainers.

The objectives and outcomes for a lesson are a bit like the rings on an archery target. The objective is the outer ring and everything in the lesson falls within this. The **All** outcome is the next ring, followed by the **Most**, and then the **Some** outcome is the bull's-eye – when the students hit this their learning really is at the centre of where you would want it to be.

Objectives and outcomes don't have to be based on knowledge and understanding – they could be based on investigation skills or on learning skills. However, you do not want to confuse the students with too many. One knowledge and understanding-based objective and one investigation skills-based objective is plenty. Each of these can then have up to three differentiated learning outcomes.

Starters

There has been much debate about whether a starter activity should be used before or after sharing the objectives and outcomes. There is no one simple answer to this. It is good practice to share the objectives and outcomes first, otherwise the students are wandering aimlessly through the starter without an outcome to head towards. However, the starter can be the place to introduce key vocabulary and the objective might not make sense without this. Alternatively, you might want to engage the students in a bit of thought around a topic, and this then might lead into the development of the objective.

A starter is more than just an introduction to the lesson; it is about engaging the students in thought to try to stimulate ideas and an interest in the next part of the lesson. The starter is also a good place to elicit the students' ideas and misconceptions about the topic of the lesson. It is therefore an important step in the learning process. A well-selected starter can help many students with SEN to make an initial step in their learning which will make the main part of the lesson more accessible.

A starter which stimulates discussion can be usefully employed for some lessons. A picture or photograph related to the topic can provide such a stimulus. For example, a lesson on forces might have a picture of a tug-of-war match, together with a list of key words: the students then have to describe the picture using as many of the key words as possible. There is an example of this type of starter on the accompanying CD (and Appendix 5.1). A lesson on diffusion might start with a demonstration of a gas jar of bromine being exposed to a gas jar of air: the students then need to describe and explain what is happening to the brown colour of the bromine.

Some of the scientific vocabulary can be confusing enough for many students but particularly so for students with SEN. Starter sessions can address the technical vocabulary which will be used in the lesson. A lesson on photosynthesis might start with the students brainstorming, or even using dictionaries to look up, as many words as possible using the prefix 'photo-'. They could then be asked to find a link between these words, leading to the idea of light. This will then help them to understand the process of photosynthesis better.

Card sorts provide a good mechanism for eliciting students' ideas and misconceptions. In a lesson on drugs, students could be asked to sort cards of different drugs to demonstrate their understanding of legality and addictiveness of these drugs. This type of activity is particularly powerful when revisited at the end of the lesson to see how the students' ideas have moved forward. There is an example of this on the accompanying CD.

The main part of the lesson

Use of DART activities

DART stands for Directed Activity Related to Text and is a useful tool to support students in translating text into other forms and thus particularly appropriate for many students with SEN. There are many different types of DART activity; we will deal with some of the main ones here.

Cloze procedures

Probably the best known of all DART activities is the cloze procedure, which usually consists of a passage of text with key words missing, and the students have to then use either their knowledge of the topic or another passage of text to fill in these missing words. Different levels of support can be given; for example, the missing words can be in a box at the top so that the students can cross these off as they complete the task, or dashes can replace the missing words to indicate the number of letters. The following example shows part of a cloze exercise related to energy transfer in food chains:

> All of the energy in a food chain originally comes from the _ _ _ .
> This energy is captured by plants through the process of _ _ _ _ _ _ _ _ _ _ _ .
> The plant is called the _ _ _ _ _ _ _ _ .
> Some animals eat only plants, they are called primary _ _ _ _ _ _ _ _ _ .
> When these animals eat the plants the _ _ _ _ _ _ is transferred to them.

Great care should be taken in the use of cloze activities. These often provide little challenge; students can sometimes guess the words to fill the gaps with little comprehension of the whole text. Cloze activities are probably best used in combination with other activities but not as the sole mechanism for learning.

Text marking

Text marking provides a relatively straightforward activity which in its simplest form avoids the need for any detailed passages of writing. This usually involves students being given a passage of text and they then underline parts of this that are related to different issues. For example, in a lesson on global warming, the students might be given a newspaper article and asked to mark this in the following ways:

- Underline in blue any part of the text which provides evidence that the Earth is warming up.

- Underline in red any part of the text which gives the causes of this warming-up.

- Underline in green any steps being taken to try to reduce this warming-up.

This can lead into the students using the parts of the text they have marked to produce their own piece of writing, possibly in a different format or genre, around the same topic. Care should be taken with the choice for the original piece of text – newspaper articles in their original form are rarely accessible to many students. These might therefore need to be translated into a more simple form of text and the use of the first person can be powerful in making text more accessible. A teaching assistant may take on this function as part of the support role.

A quick assessment of the reading level of a piece of text can be obtained using the SMOG formula (see Appendix 5.2).

Diagram and text completion

Diagram completion or labelling can provide an effective way of checking student understanding of a passage of text and giving them a useful way of recording the main points from this. The students are given a passage of text and asked to use this to label or complete a diagram. For example, they might be given a passage on the structure of plant cells and they might use this to label a diagram showing the different parts of a plant cell. You might combine this activity with text marking to provide an interim step to make this activity more accessible.

Text completion involves giving the students the start to a sentence or paragraph and then asking them to complete it. For example, when studying electrical circuits, you might ask them to complete a passage of text which starts:

> In our first circuit, the bulb was lit because . . .
> In our second circuit, the two bulbs were dim because . . .

Clearly, text completion can be set at a relatively high level of demand, as to complete the sentences above fully would require an understanding of complete circuits and of current being shared between bulbs. Students might need two or three attempts at these to include enough detail.

Text matching

Text matching is similar to text completion but made easier by the fact that the second part of the sentence is provided. This means that rather than having to think of the reasons, the students just need to identify the correct option. So, in a text matching exercise which includes the two sentence starters above, among the sentence endings might be:

> . . . there is a complete circuit, with no gaps in it.
> . . . the electric current from the cell is shared between the two bulbs.

Sentence ordering

Sentence ordering is an exercise which can be used to help students make sense of a passage of text. The passage is divided up into sentences, and the students are then presented with these as a series of cards which they need then to place into the correct order. For example, when studying solar eclipses, the students could be given sentences which describe a viewer's observations during an eclipse and be asked to place these into chronological order. This exercise might be taken to the next level by asking the students to describe why these phenomena were observed at each point in terms of the relative positions of the three bodies involved.

True/false exercises

Maybe one of the simplest forms of DART exercise is a true/false exercise. Students are given a series of statements and they simply have to state whether these are true or false. This could be for series of statements about the function of specialised plant cells, for example. In other examples where the evidence is less clear-cut, the students might be asked to decide whether they agree or disagree, and this could then lead into discussions about the topic. Examples of this type of activity are included on the accompanying CD.

Word puzzles

There are various forms of word puzzle that can be used. The most common are crosswords and wordsearches, which can be particularly useful in developing students' recognition of key vocabulary. A crossword of circuit symbols could be used where the students are given the symbols as the clues and have to write the names in the crossword grid. A wordsearch of different types of food could be given to the students: not only could they identify the words but they could colour-code the different food groups. For example, they could shade all of the foods which are a good source of protein in red.

These are just some of the forms of the DART approach. It is important to try to match the form of activity to the topic and to the students so that they can achieve success. It is also important that you use a mix of different activities to provide variety; if you gave out a cloze exercise every lesson the students would soon become bored.

Learning styles and multiple intelligences

The American psychologist Howard Gardner, in his seminal 1993 work *Frames of Mind: Theory of Multiple Intelligences* and in his 2000 revisit of his original work in *Intelligence Reframed: Multiple Intelligences for the 21st Century*, describes what has come to be known as 'multiple intelligences'. Gardner has defined eight main intelligences, and these are:

- **Linguistic intelligence**: this is demonstrated by skill with both spoken and written language, sometimes involving the ability to learn foreign languages, and usually coupled with the ability to use language well to achieve certain objectives.

- **Logical–mathematical intelligence**: this is demonstrated by an ability to approach and analyse problems in a logical way, usually shown through an ability to carry out mathematical operations and often a systematic approach to scientific enquiry.

- **Musical intelligence**: this is demonstrated by skill in composition and performance of music as well as by an appreciation of music and an understanding of the patterns within it.

- **Bodily–kinaesthetic intelligence**: this is shown by the use of the body, either as a whole or in part, to solve problems or create products; it is often displayed by good aptitude in sports or in crafts.

- **Spatial intelligence**: this is the potential to visualise solutions and patterns either over a large area or in a more confined space, and it can be displayed as good map-reading skills, the ability to see a finished sculpture from a block of wood or the ability to play chess well.

- **Interpersonal intelligence**: this is the ability to understand and empathise with the desires and intentions of other people.

- **Intrapersonal intelligence**: this is the ability to understand one's own desires, fears and capabilities.

- **Naturalist intelligence**: in its strictest definition, this is demonstrated by an ability to recognise and classify species of plants and animals; however, it can also be demonstrated by an ability to recognise and classify almost anything, for example recognising the make and model of a motorcycle by the sound of its engine.

In identifying these eight intelligences, Gardner has done more than just observe and test people; he has backed his arguments up with a series of criteria for judging whether an 'intelligence' exists or not. Whilst it is not possible to map each intelligence to one particular part of the brain, Gardner has demonstrated that patients with brain damage can show the loss of one or more of these types of intelligence. These intelligences do not occur singularly: most people display varying amounts of each of these. However, one or more of these intelligences can be more highly developed than the others, and this is often shown by students displaying particular 'talents'.

At this stage you might be asking yourself how this applies to teaching science to students with special educational needs. An understanding of the principle of multiple intelligences makes the choice of activities for the class you are to teach more focused. For example, students with autistic spectrum disorder often have under-developed interpersonal intelligence and find group work difficult. However, these same students can show highly developed naturalist intelligence, which means that when it comes to work on classification they whizz through the topic. Students with ASD can also show highly developed logical–mathematical intelligence, which means that they are superb at solving problems and undertaking scientific investigations; however, they often have under-developed linguistic intelligence and hence have difficulty recording their ideas. Students who suffer from Down syndrome often have poorly developed logical–mathematical, linguistic and bodily–kinaesthetic intelligences but can have highly developed musical intelligence.

Almost all of the students you will teach will have at least one of these intelligences which is more developed than the others. The problem is that the traditional education system is built around students using mainly linguistic and logical–mathematical intelligences. It is also these two intelligences by which students are usually examined. Those students who appear to 'fail' in the education system often do so because they are effectively square pegs in round holes in terms of the way they are being asked to learn and in the way they are examined.

It is not possible to provide eight different learning activities, one for each of the different intelligences, in any one lesson. When you differentiate the work, if you did this at three levels this would mean 24 activities in just one lesson, which is clearly not possible. However, it is possible to give a range of activities over a series of lessons so that each student can experience success. This does require the teacher to be a bit more imaginative when devising activities. To have been successful in science education, the teacher will probably have a highly developed logical–mathematical intelligence but might find it hard to think in the same way as someone who has a highly developed bodily–kinaesthetic or musical intelligence.

It is important to consider which part of the lesson contains the stage where the students develop their ideas most. In a practical lesson this is often the stage where the students write their conclusions. Traditionally, we ask students to write a two-paragraph conclusion, one describing the pattern and giving the evidence for this, the second explaining these observations in terms of the scientific ideas. This approach works well for students with highly developed linguistic intelligence but less well for the others. We could at this stage give the students a range of options to present their ideas, such as bullet-pointed lists, concept maps, diagrams and maybe even putting their ideas into a rap. These all require very different skills and we cannot expect students to use these straight away – they need to experience and learn each of these techniques and then develop the one(s) which work best for them. We do, however, need to bear in mind that sometimes the students will have to present their ideas as two paragraphs of text, for example in GCSE coursework, so occasionally we do need to teach this skill and let them practise it.

Modelling

Science is full of models, be they physical models or intellectual ones. All too often we present a model as fact, often confusing students either with this initial model or later when we have to replace it with a more sophisticated one. We need at every stage to share with the students what we are doing in terms of the models and to consider their limitations. Let us consider how we might develop a model of particles as an example:

Initial model – marbles in a tray, to consider how particles move compared with their internal energy.

Second model – use of coloured polystyrene balls to represent atoms, joining two or more together to form molecules.

Third model – use of particle model kits to illustrate the number of bonds each atom can form and to develop molecular formulae.

Final model – some students might go on and consider electron orbits in shells, then refine this to consider 'p' and 's' shells, etc. If they really take their scientific studies to the highest levels, they might consider the orbits in terms of probability of where the electrons might lie and even consider wave–particle duality.

None of these models gives an exact description of how particles appear and behave. Each one is, however, a 'good enough' model at each stage in the students' cognitive development. It is therefore important to treat the models as such. For some students with special educational needs models work well: they make a theoretical idea such as particles more tangible and concrete. For other students, however, the model becomes the concept, and therefore particles might be made of glass with coloured bits in the middle and be the size of marbles. It is therefore more important for students with special educational needs than for most to consider which models to use and when to use them. For some students, such as those with Asperger syndrome, this type of physical model can help them to grasp abstract concepts.

Similar considerations need to be made with physical models. A typical homework might be to make a model of a cell of your choice. These models will then be displayed and even house points given out to the best ones, a great activity for students with highly developed bodily–kinaesthetic and spatial intelligences. However, the problem is in deciding which the best ones are. For example, a plastic bag filled with water with a coloured marble floating in it might look good as an animal cell but this can lead to misconceptions, in this case particularly that the cell membrane is impermeable. On the other hand, a teabag which has been slit open, a Smartie placed inside and then sewn back together might not look very attractive but better represents the semi-permeable nature of the cell membrane. In using physical models, therefore, it is important to consider their limitations as well as ways in which they are good at representing reality. Care also needs to be taken that the model does not replace the reality for some students with special educational needs.

Scientific enquiry

Investigation skills form the backbone of scientific discovery: in teaching these we are equipping the students to be real scientists and to give them the facility to solve their own scientific problems. All too often we assume that the students acquire the skills by undertaking investigations, and it is less usual for the individual investigation skills to be taught. This is of particular importance when teaching some students with special educational needs for whom small steps in developing learning and skills is the best approach.

It is important to give the students ownership of the investigation and to relate this to everyday life. If you introduce the investigation by simply telling the class that they are going to investigate how the temperature of the water affects how much sugar will dissolve in it, they are not performing their own investigation; they are performing yours. Planning posters can be useful here. By starting with an open question, such as 'What affects sugar dissolving?', the students can suggest and develop their own ideas. These ideas might be many moved forward. In the card sorts on drugs, they might have sorted the cards into 'Legal', 'Illegal' and 'Not sure'. After the main part of the lesson they may want to add another category 'Controlled', and some of the drugs which might have been in other categories can now be moved into this one, demonstrating new understanding.

Performing a plenary is not quite the end of the story. When the lesson has ended, you need a few moments to reflect on the students' learning and to decide where to go next. If the objective of the lesson was for the students to accurately define the terms 'atom' and 'element' and in a plenary the students have clearly shown that they do not have an understanding of these two terms, then there is no way that you can go on to the next lesson on molecules and compounds. Most schemes of work contain a series of lessons which contain ideas which build on each other. It is not good practice to mindlessly teach lesson 1, followed by lesson 2, followed by lesson 3, etc., unless the students have grasped the ideas from the previous lesson. You might need to revisit the objective with a different activity to try to move the students' learning forward.

Use of homework

Before setting homework, you need to consider such questions as 'Is this homework really appropriate for this group?', 'What benefit will these students gain from undertaking this piece of homework?' For some students, such as those with ADHD, routine is important, so if homework is regularly set on a certain night of the week, then it may be best to stick to this. There are positive reasons to set homework – it can be used to:

- develop skills used in the lesson

- reinforce some of the ideas from the lesson

- test knowledge gained

- develop key vocabulary

- give opportunities for independent research

- allow pupils time to plan and carry out surveys

- put the learning into context in the home

- allow the application of ideas to new situations by using problem-solving skills.

Homework can become a real barrier and for some an area of failure. If a student is consistently not completing homework and getting into trouble the following lesson, this barrier to learning will then overflow into lesson time. Other students may achieve a high level of success within the lesson but if inappropriate homework is set then this might temper that success. It is therefore important to set differentiated homework, especially for those students who will not have any support at home. For students with disabilities which make them more tired than most, you need to consider the amount of homework with which they have to cope. In a class which contains students with special educational needs, it is also important to consider when to set the homework; for example, if you set this in the last two minutes of the lesson (as many teachers do), do these students have time to record what they have to do and check if they do not understand?

Appendix 5.3 gives three examples of different styles of homework that could be used with pupils with varying special needs. One considers key words; the second is a research technique that could be used; the third looks at writing an experimental report.

Conclusion

If there were one simple answer to how to teach science as effectively as possible, then someone would have discovered this by now and would probably have retired on the profits. However, structuring your lessons carefully and planning these around the objectives will certainly get you on the right track. Variety is also important: one of the misconceptions about the key stage 3 Strategy is that it dictates that every lesson should be a 'three-part lesson' – this is not true. What it does suggest, however, is that most lessons can be broken down into learning episodes, and this is particularly important when teaching students with special educational needs. Short sharp activities are invariably better than long drawn-out ones. Appendix 5.4 can be used and shared with other teachers as a reminder of the main principles of lesson planning.

Every child and every class is different, and it is not therefore possible to pull standard lessons off the shelf and assume that they will work. You need to consider how to modify certain tasks for certain students and present an appropriate level of challenge to move their learning forward, but at the same time any task must not be so difficult that not only will they fail. To quote Sotto (1997):

> To teach in a way which takes account of the way people learn requires systematic study of how they learn followed by a great many struggles to translate such study into effective practice.

pictures and correct writing into their books. This indicates their understanding and not their writing skill.

- Using a tape recorder for homework can be a useful alternative to writing down results. For instance, at key stage 4 when writing the results for an experiment after testing urine (obviously artificial, cold tea with chemicals added is a wonderful substitute!), a pupil could record their findings and also explain their conclusion. If it is really necessary for them to have notes, you could then photocopy someone else's notes for them because you know they understand the science of how kidneys function.

- Listening to pupils talking among themselves about the work gives an insight into individual understanding. This can be done in formal or informal settings. Again, if you are considering fuels at key stage 3, by setting up a class debate with every pupil having a part to play it is possible to assess the progress of pupils with special educational needs. Be sure to allow sufficient planning and rehearsal time – providing a speaking frame can also be useful.

- Another useful method when assessing progress could be to ask everyone in the class to write a mnemonic. The obvious use of a mnemonic is when remembering the colours of the spectrum or the order of the planets, but they can be used equally successfully for remembering other specific details. Often, the pupils will suggest them as a way of remembering facts – get the mnemonic right and you know instantly whether they have grasped a particular concept or fact.

- The use of simple tunes is another way pupils can show their understanding. Key stage 4 work about electrical circuits has some possibilities. If they put *resistance equals voltage divided by current* to a simple or popular tune, such as one for an advertisement, and they then either tape them or repeat them next lesson, it is easier for students to remember and apply such concepts.

- As the pupil completes practical work, using a digital camera to photograph them can be valuable. Also using a video camera and playing it back so they can see how they perform a particular experiment can be a valuable tool, although there is the issue of confidentiality and written permission is required to photograph or film pupils. When developing the skill of using a measuring cylinder at key stage 3, a teaching aid can be created by photographing pupils using one to point out any mistakes (such as not getting their eye level with the meniscus or tipping the measuring cylinder).

- Using True/False or Yes/No cards as a whole group to answer simple questions shows the level of understanding of scientific concepts within a group. Noticing who is looking round and copying others indicates how confident they are and where their knowledge is lacking. It is important to use follow-up questions such as 'What reasons do you have for answering 'False' to that question?' This can be a useful starter or plenary, especially at key stage 3. For example, it can be used to test their understanding of particles and how they behave in solids, liquids and gases.

● For assessment to be of value there needs to be feedback given to the pupils. Again, the method may vary from speaking individually with a pupil to asking the whole group. This is a valuable method after group presentations and can lead to raising the self-esteem of pupils if the feedback is constructive.

Whatever method is employed, the pupils need to feel it is a fair process and it is important to link the feedback, either verbal or written, to the learning objectives set at the outset of the lesson. For example, if the learning objective is to understand displacement reactions and the pupil has obviously not understood that they are dependent on the reactivity of the metals used, it is not acceptable just to indicate their answers are wrong. They also need to know that the more reactive metal displaces the less reactive metal; without this knowledge they will never understand displacement reactions.

Formally recording progress also needs consideration. When marking tests at both key stages, writing the mark alone can be unhelpful. Giving comments which relate to progress against individual targets is far more supportive, as is helpful advice about exactly how to do better next time. The pupils then know how they are performing and where improvements need to be made. For instance, they may have just completed a unit containing ideas about photosynthesis and their test indicates they have failed to understand that oxygen is given off as a by-product of the reaction. Their next unit may contain work about respiration and by having the teacher's comment about oxygen, they will find the next unit easier to understand.

How do teachers record the results? Are these fed back to a centrally held database for the faculty? This is an excellent way of tracking the progress of pupils: it allows comparisons between individual pupils and allows tracking of pupils' individual progress over the whole of a key stage.

As the SAT papers are returned to schools, these can be used to assess the quality of the teaching for the different units. Although this process takes time, it is time well spent as the information it gives to the teacher is invaluable.

A TABLE TO HELP MONITOR SAT RESULTS FOR A GROUP

Set _____	Record of Marks for Science SAT Paper 1								Total number of marks (140)
Name of pupil	Question number and number of marks for each question								
	1 (5)	2 (6)	3 (3)	4 (6)	5 (4)	6 (3)	7 (5)	etc.	

The use of the Pupil Achievement Tracker (PAT) can also generate invaluable information to identify pupils' needs and support future learning. It can also be useful for target setting. (Regular updates are available on the Standards website: www.standards.dfes.gov.uk.)

This sort of analysis highlights the strengths and weaknesses of pupils and can be a valuable tool for the science teacher, especially when comparing pupils with a particular special need to their peers and deciding on the best course for them at key stage 4. It also allows the science teacher to report accurately to the SEN faculty.

These tables could also be modified to use for recording grades for end-of-unit tests. As they are easy to set up and save on a computer, and spreadsheets can do all the calculations if required, useful information can be stored and used to monitor pupils. Other details, such as estimated grades or actual grades, could also be included. By using a standard format, a blank document can be stored and then used for a variety of record-keeping and can ensure the faculty is working together. It is also useful for tracking pupils, including those with SEN, throughout a key stage. The table below shows how this might be done.

A TABLE TO MONITOR THE PROGRESS OF PUPILS THROUGH A KEY STAGE

Set _____	Record of Marks								Overall level for the year
Name of pupil	Unit number and marks for that unit								
	1 (25)	2 (25)	3 (25)	4 (25)	5 (25)	6 (25)	7 (25)	etc.	

A number of useful methods can be used when recording assessments for practical work. A can-do test method can be used: if the teacher observes a pupil handling a piece of apparatus correctly, a tick is placed by their name. This helps to build up a picture of their capabilities with practical work. This is particularly important if they have fine or gross motor skill problems. Taking a video clip of them working can also be valuable for this type of pupil but it is important to remember that some pupils will be embarrassed or feel nervous. In such circumstances, using the video camera with the whole group could make a difference so they do not feel singled out. If they still find the method embarrassing, consider other methods.

A simple grid can be used when recording scientific enquiry work, such as bit tasks or whole investigations (which are marked to National Curriculum levels). For most pupils just the level for the skill can be used, but finer detail may be required to show progress for some pupils with special educational needs, and this requires careful consideration. The table below gives one way this may be done.

MONITORING SCIENTIFIC ENQUIRY SKILLS WITHIN A KEY STAGE

Science group:		Scientific enquiry skills			
Title of work	Name of pupil	Planning and predicting	Obtaining evidence	Analysing results	Evaluating

By considering the nature of the task set, it may be possible to record small steps that the pupil has gained, rather than just level at key stage 3 or the mark if it is key stage 4. Although levels and marks are important, for some pupils more detailed records may be of greater value to show progression.

Recording results for pupils with poor motor skills

A Year 7 group is following QCA unit 7A – Cells. They are considering plant and animal cells and are introduced to the idea that there are differences between plant and animal cells. They are provided with a labelled diagram of an animal cell and shown how to make a plant cell slide from an onion. They have previously used a microscope to look at a variety of objects to see how it can be used to give information about structure. Initially they have to write down what they would do and then carry out the experiment, recording their results.

Within the group is a pupil with cerebral palsy who finds using apparatus difficult but who has a TA present. A sheet like the table below could be used. The TA could fill in the sections and if the pupil correctly knows how to make the slide the TA could tick the box. By using this sort of table, small areas of improvement can be noticed and recorded.

TABLE TO MONITOR PROGRESS OF A PUPIL WITH CEREBRAL PALSY

Name of pupil:		Scientific enquiry skills			
Title of practical work	Planning and predicting	Obtaining evidence	Analysing results	Evaluating
What are the differences between a plant and animal cell?	Lists apparatus needed	Gives instructions to partner to make the slide accurately	Tells TA what to draw after viewing plant slide	Can clearly state how to make an improvement to the experiment
	Sequences stages for making the slide	Tells partner how to set up the microscope	Tells TA what to draw when viewing animal slide	
	Gives a safety point		Can say two differences between slides	

Contributing to reviews

Many teachers in secondary schools are unaware of the detailed SEN reporting procedures within a school. However, with a greater knowledge of the reporting system for SEN pupils, the science faculty can supply key information about individual pupils. Such detailed records as mentioned above can be invaluable when, for example, writing a report for the SEN team for the annual review for a pupil with motor skill problems.

It is therefore helpful to have an understanding of the type of reporting system for SEN required within your school. A science teacher will be able to make a valuable contribution to annual reviews as well as IEPs written for specific pupils. This is where having a designated member of staff linking with the SEN department becomes useful. They can explain to the other science teachers the type of information required and the depth of detail to be included.

The SEN department usually has a standard form when asking teachers to report back for annual reviews and when making comments for the review of IEPs. This enables relevant information to be collected in a unified manner. You may be asked throughout the year to comment about the following, depending on the purpose of the enquiry:

- how well the pupil is working towards their IEP targets

- their positive achievements within your subject

- how your course is differentiated to suit their requirements

- how practical work is differentiated and whether adapted apparatus is used

- the way in which the support provided by the SEN department is used within the lesson

- whether they are achieving their curriculum target

- how they can make further progress within your subject

- how they are coping with social skills.

This is the generic information required from all subjects, but the nature of science means that useful information can be provided about their practical skills. It is possible to comment on a pupil's ability to pour from containers and the adaptations required, such as using a funnel or a piece of non-slip matting, that it would be impossible to comment about in other subjects. Simple can-do tests provide useful measures of progress and can help to build students' confidence.

MONITORING SCIENTIFIC ENQUIRY AT KEY STAGE 4

Name: Class: I can:	Date observed, and detail of task
light a Bunsen burner	
adjust a Bunsen burner to make a blue flame	
measure the volume of a liquid	
use a microscope	
heat a test tube in a flame	
find the pH of a liquid	
use a spatula	
measure the temperature of a liquid	
filter a mixture	
time how long a reaction takes	
use a retort stand	
measure the mass of an object	
set up a circuit with a bulb	
measure the current in a circuit	
measure the voltage of a cell	
count the number of beats of a pulse in a minute	

National Curriculum levels and P scales

Key stage 3

The National Curriculum clearly sets out levels 1–8 and at the end of key stage 3 a level for scientific enquiry will be required as well as one for knowledge and understanding. Some pupils may not be working within these levels, however, and P levels (performance descriptors outlining attainment before National Curriculum level 1) can be used both to report progress and to effectively differentiate work set.

There are 8 performance descriptors in the P scale and these are applied like the National Curriculum level descriptors. The first three are cross-curricular. These are:

- P1 (i) – Pupils encounter activities and experiences.

- P1 (ii) – Pupils show emerging awareness of activities and experiences.

- P2 (i) – Pupils begin to respond consistently to familiar people, events and objects.

- P2 (ii) – Pupils begin to be proactive in their interactions.

- P3 (i) – Pupils begin to communicate intentionally.

- P3 (ii) – Pupils use emerging conversational communication.

From level P4 to P8 it is possible to describe pupils' performance in a way that indicates the emergence of skills, knowledge and understanding in science, as outlined below.
P4 pupils:

- explore objects and materials, changing their properties by physical means and observing the outcomes, e.g. mixing flour and water.

- know that certain actions produce predictable results.

- can communicate their awareness of changes in light, sound or movement.

- imitate movements and sounds.

- show interest in a wide range of living things, e.g. by collecting items from a walk in the woods.

P5 pupils:

- anticipate and join in activities focused on enquiry into specific environments, e.g. finding the hamster under the straw.

- group objects and materials in terms of simple features or properties.

- indicate the before and after of material changes.

- engage in experimentation with a range of equipment in familiar and relevant situations, e.g. initiating the activation of a range of light sources.

- answer simple scientific questions, such as 'Where is the flower?', 'Is it hot or cold?'

P6 pupils:

- explore objects and materials provided in an appropriate way.

- recognise features of objects, and know where they belong, e.g. leaves on a tree.

- begin to make generalisations, connections and predictions from regular experience.

- consistently sort materials according to given criteria when the contrast is obvious.

- closely observe changes that occur.

- can identify some appliances that use electricity, and can recall the sources of sound and light.

P7 pupils:

- actively join in scientific investigations.

- understand simple scientific vocabulary and communicate related ideas and observations using simple phrases.

- can sort materials reliably with given criteria.

- observe some of the simple properties of light, sound and movement.

- begin to record their findings.

- begin to make suggestions for planning and evaluating their work.

P8 pupils:

- explore and observe similarities, differences, patterns and changes in features of objects, living things and events.

- begin to make their own contributions to planning and evaluation and to record their findings in different ways.

- can identify a range of common materials and know about some of their properties.

- can sort materials using simple criteria and can communicate observations of materials in terms of these properties.

- make observations of changes in light, sound or movement that result from actions, e.g. pressing a switch.

- describe changes when questioned directly.

Key stage 4

The QCA guidance (QCA, 2001:26) for key stage 4 is: 'The focus of teaching science at key stage 4 may be on giving pupils opportunities to:

- apply their knowledge, skills and experience in new situations.

- consider explanations and the causation of things around them, their bodies and events.'

Some pupils with SEN are quite capable of completing double science courses. Others will need some adapted materials or support. It is important to sort out the needs of the pupils and apply for any special arrangements well before the exam process begins. For other students, there are alternative accreditation opportunities. Recent proposals for greater curriculum flexibility and choice for young people aged 14–16 have been welcomed by teachers and senior decision-makers, as is the emphasis on science related to everyday contexts as a way of providing a more relevant and motivating core for most students.

Pupils at key stage 4 who operate within the National Curriculum assessment levels 1–3 may follow courses leading to accreditation for an 'entry level in science'. Those operating above level 3 may follow a syllabus leading to potential accreditation for a GCSE in science. For further information contact the awarding bodies listed below.

AQA: www.aqa.org.uk/qual/vgcse/sci.html

Edexcel: www.edexcel.org.uk/quals

OCR: www.ocr.org.uk

QCA: www.qca.org.uk/3186.html

A comprehensive list of examination boards is available at www.teachersweb. co.uk/teach/teach_exam.html.

Conclusion

The science faculty may need to adapt and adjust information for the SEN department within a school for the variety of reports and assessments that have to be completed. Having one named science teacher for liaison with the SEN department can be especially helpful in this regard.

Assessment, if used in a positive manner with pupils with special educational needs, can be of great value. It is important to acknowledge and praise even the smallest achievements in order to build pupils' self-esteem and keep them motivated.

For some pupils, the smallest step represents a huge effort – teachers need to recognise this and reward accordingly.

CHAPTER 7

Managing Support

One of the main principles laid out in the *Special Educational Needs Code of Practice* is that:

> For the vast majority of children their mainstream setting will meet all their special educational needs. Some children will require additional help from SEN services or other agencies external to the school.

> (DfES 2001:1)

This principle has a bearing on every science faculty and their provision for students with SEN, especially as there is a move towards more inclusive schools. Consideration will need to be given to different support strategies and how they can be structured to meet the individual needs of students within the context of science lessons.

Teaching assistants (TAs) are increasing in number and workforce remodelling continues to re-define and develop their roles. There is also a move to train TAs in specific areas of the curriculum and some schools have been using this approach for a while. This moves TAs away from supporting particular pupils in all subjects to working more closely within a faculty and developing subject knowledge as well as establishing sound working relationships with subject staff. It may be more difficult to put in place where TAs are part of the support detailed in a pupil's Statement of SEN, as these often specify a number of hours of support for the pupil and 'lock in' the TA to accompanying the pupil to a range of lessons. In this situation, the TA can be expected to have good knowledge of the pupils and their particular needs, but less knowledge of science.

In large secondary schools, there is likely to be a blend of these two approaches. There may also be peripatetic teachers from pupil support teams who are allocated some time to work with a particular pupil and who may also act in an advisory capacity to support the teacher.

Whatever the nature of support in science lessons, it is important for the teacher to manage the learning environment and the other adults in it. The responsibility for every pupil's learning, behaviour and achievement lies with the teacher.

It is the teacher whose curriculum and lesson planning and day-to-day direction set the framework within which the teaching/classroom assistants work. The TA works under the direction of the teacher, whether in the whole class or on their own with an individual or a small group of pupils. TAs therefore need to be fully briefed about the teacher's plans and intentions for teaching and learning and her/his contribution to these. Ideally, teaching/classroom assistants will be involved by teachers in their planning and preparation of the work.

(LGNTO, *Teaching/Classroom Assistants National Occupational Standards*, 2001)

Having a clear idea of the role of TAs and what they are expected to achieve is fundamental to making the best use of their support. Each local authority has its guidelines regarding TAs and *Working with Teaching Assistants* (DfEE, 2000) is a useful document. Both these form a good backbone for developing the right ethos about support within the school and the science faculty. The National Standards for TAs can also be useful in defining a school's or a department's expectations (www.lg-employers.gov.uk).

As a faculty, it is important to look at the SEN policy once a year and if necessary ask the SENCO to attend the meeting so that any concerns can be discussed. This will enable staff to have shared objectives when teaching pupils with SEN and there will be better continuity. It is valuable for the faculty to have their own SEN policy statement, setting out clear objectives that are annually reviewed. These could include:

- that all science teachers are responsible for meeting the needs of the pupils they teach.

- working with TAs and how they are included within the faculty.

- a reminder about confidentiality.

- linking with the SEN department and where to gain information.

- using IEPs as working documents.

- an update on adapted apparatus and differentiated worksheets.

Types of support

There are a number of ways in which a TA can provide support:

- **Support the teacher**
  If the TA works with individual students on a regular basis, she/he is likely to know the sort of difficulties which might be encountered in science lessons – and how to avoid or overcome them. The TA could suggest ways of adapting apparatus. For example, a student with a visual impairment might need big numbers on a measuring cylinder in black permanent ink. The TA may also be able to modify and simplify printed material and recording sheets to make them more accessible to individual pupils (see below).

- **Support a student**

  For example, if the group are looking at the difference between series and parallel circuits and comparing the effect on three light bulbs, the TA could help to set up the experiment and prepare a way for the pupil to record the results – this might be a simple recording format, a digital photograph or an audio recording. There are important considerations to be made about this type of support and the way it is delivered so that students do not feel stigmatised and different from the rest of the group.

- **Support a group of students**

  Imagine that the science teacher has just instructed the whole class to work in groups to find the most acidic household chemical from a range provided; they have to add universal indicator from a dropping bottle and then compare the colours to a pH chart. In a situation such as this, the TA could work within an area of the laboratory, ensuring that pupils have understood what they have to do, checking safety arrangements and improving their understanding of the science involved. Keeping pupils on task, structuring the work and encouraging them to think about what is happening are all valuable parts of a support role.

- **Support the curriculum**

  Consider the situation where a key stage 4 group are planning an experiment to look at osmosis using potatoes. This requires knowledge of cells. If the TA knows the syllabus, she/he can remind the students about previous work, making links within the curriculum. Similarly, a TA who has worked with a pupil in other areas of the curriculum can act as a 'bridge' between subjects, emphasising common areas and reminding pupils of, for example, numerical operations learned.

MODIFYING WORKSHEETS

- Use a simple, uncluttered layout and leave a wide margin around the page.

- Use a large font size – 14 pt or larger. Experiment with different styles to find out which is easiest for pupils to read.

- Use different colours of paper – pastel shades are often easier to read than black ink on white paper.

- Use subheadings to structure the text and help the reader.

- Break up the text into short chunks or paragraphs; use boxes and bullet points.

- Make use of illustrations if they are helpful to the reader – avoid using them for decoration.

- Separate illustrations/diagrams/tables from the text.

- Avoid double columns of text – make it clear where the reader has to start reading each section.

- Use simple and familiar language. Keep sentences short and concise. Use the first person where possible.

- Highlight and explain key words and any new terminology.

Training of teaching assistants

Margerison (1997) highlighted the value of giving training to TAs and with the introduction of higher-level TAs a range of courses has recently become available to develop their skills. One resource which is particularly useful is the 'Induction Training for Teaching Assistants in Secondary Schools – Science Module' (reference DfES/0584/2004).

Talking to the TAs will enable science teachers to gain a greater knowledge of the skills they already have and where there are opportunities for further development.

It is important that the support staff are aware of the ethos behind science teaching. Apart from a knowledge of the actual courses used within the faculty, a basic background of the National Curriculum is very useful.

THE NATIONAL CURRICULUM FOR SCIENCE

The National Curriculum consists of four attainment targets for all key stages. These are:

- Sc 1 Scientific Enquiry
- Sc 2 Life Processes and Living Things
- Sc 3 Materials and Their Properties
- Sc 4 Physical Processes

For each key stage there is:

- a programme of study
- attainment targets
- level descriptors

There are six key skills embodied within the National Curriculum:

- communication
- application of number
- use of ICT
- working with others
- improving own learning and performance
- problem-solving

There are an additional five skills embedded within the National Curriculum, which may have particular significance for pupils with special needs; all of them have some bearing on the teaching of science:

- physical, orientation and mobility skills
- organisation and study skills
- personal and social skills
- daily living skills
- leisure and recreational skills.

Certain skills are required by the TAs, such as the use of questioning to develop the scientific knowledge and the confidence of the student. The use of questioning is a skill which plays a vital part in the learning of science and TAs need confidence and training in this. Development of good questioning skills within students is also a key skill in developing effective scientists. For any student it is essential to guide them to making sensible choices by using clear language rather than making the choice for them. It is important to know:

- Why are questions asked?

- What are the different types of question?

- How do you ask questions?

- How to decide on the best question?

- How do you re-frame questions?

The last point needs some further clarity between the TA and teacher, and this is where forward planning is useful because if the TA knows the objectives for the lesson, she/he can rc form the question for the student without giving the answer.

It is also important to develop the practical skills of the TAs, and running training sessions for them can enhance their skills. As part of faculty development, training in the use of equipment, especially ICT equipment such as dataloggers and temperature probes, should be a matter of course. It is therefore important to ensure that support staff have a basic scientific knowledge and an understanding of the way to handle equipment. This could be done individually with the TA for your lesson or considered as part of the development of the learning support staff and science faculty staff through work on training days. Appendix 7.2 gives a useful summary sheet for training purposes.

Planning support

Within the science laboratory it is vital that the science teacher and the TA work together. For this to be most effective it is important that TAs:

- clearly know in advance the objectives, learning outcomes, content of the lesson and any experiments.

- be able to discuss how the work could be differentiated for a particular student or group of students and who will make the adjustments to worksheets, etc.

- and the teacher use each other's expertise to develop the skills of the student – the TA may have greater understanding of a particular student's needs.

- prior to the lesson decide whether the student needs time for reinforcement of basic scientific concepts rather than learning a number of new concepts.

- consider whether they will write notes and/or record results for the student to enable them to focus on the scientific concepts.

- decide whether the homework will be differentiated by content or outcome.

- know where to sit/stand during the lesson.

- decide how the students they support will be grouped within the room.

Some of these may seem obvious, but the simplest point can become overlooked and the quality of the support jeopardised.

It is also important that the TA has an adequate scientific knowledge to enable the students requiring support to have their learning extended. It is not good enough to have the situation where the TA is learning the scientific skills at the same time as the student. If they are to successfully support the student they will need to:

- have a good knowledge of safety rules within the laboratory.

- be confident in handling simple apparatus such as Bunsen burners and measuring cylinders.

- be familiar with where apparatus is stored within the laboratory.

- know how to draw basic tables, charts and graphs.

- be able to use ICT equipment such as temperature probes, etc.

- be familiar with how to complete and record an investigation.

- know where adapted apparatus and worksheets are stored.

Medium-term planning is important for any science teacher aiming to be well-organised. It enables you to decide if you need to book any specialist equipment or adapt any worksheets or apparatus. It is at this stage that the involvement of support staff can be usefully included. They may be able to suggest practical work that may be more successful for particular students or ways of adapting worksheets and differentiating work that will enrich the curriculum for those students with special educational needs. Appendix 7.3 gives an example of a planning sheet that can be used.

Short-term planning is important for ordering apparatus and checking work with the support staff. This could be recorded in a diary or kept in a book. Appendix 7.4 has a simple chart for this type of record-keeping.

Appendix 7.5 contains an example of a planning sheet that could be used by TAs within science. As a school policy, encouraging TAs to use a diary for recording the type of support they offer and adaptations to work made for students could be a valuable record for future referral. At faculty meetings, this information could be shared and alterations to resources and schemes of work could be made if necessary.

Allow time to discuss the short-term planning with TAs, by providing them with the actual plan for a unit of work and asking them for ideas and ways of differentiating aspects of it to suit the students they support. This also allows them the opportunity to attend the lessons fully prepared and rightly makes them feel valued.

The support from the TA does not end when the lesson ends. The TA is a valuable source of feedback on how well the students met the learning outcomes. This can be used to evaluate the success of the lesson and in particular to evaluate the strategies used with the students being supported. Furthermore, it can help to determine not only suitable outcomes for the next lesson but also to refine how support is used.

Welding, when writing about in-class support, indicated the value of working together:

> Good support teaching is all about good staff teamwork, through which the teachers bring different skills and strengths to the lesson.
>
> (Welding 1996)

Conclusion

- Include the management of TAs in all lesson planning. Be sure about what you want them to do and be clear about expected outcomes.

- Consider the most effective use of TAs. Can some of their time be spent supporting students out of the laboratory or preparing resources?

- Use the TAs' knowledge of particular students and their likely difficulties in certain science lessons to pre-empt possible barriers to learning.

- Encourage TAs to access information regarding special adaptations that could be valuable within the laboratory setting.

- Develop the TAs' scientific skills and ensure they have a basic knowledge of science and safety aspects of the subject.

- Include the TAs in the discipline procedure within the laboratory and provide them with training about when it would be appropriate to intervene.

CHAPTER 8

Real Pupils in Real Classrooms

Eight case studies have been included in this chapter to describe real pupils in science lessons. They may be useful for discussion in departmental training and/or act as a starting point for planning appropriately for similar pupils in your own school. The lesson plans are included on the accompanying CD for you to download and amend as necessary.

Individual Education Plans (IEPs) are usually designed by the SENCO or a member of the learning support team for pupils who are at School Action Plus, or who have a Statement of SEN. These will often describe generic targets to do with literacy, social skills and behaviour. It is important that science teachers take note of these targets and incorporate them into their planning. For example, if a pupil's target is to learn to read and spell five new words every week, some of those words could be linked to science. If a target is to 'stay on task' for ten minutes at a time, the science teacher and/or the TA can observe the pupil's behaviour in science lessons and report back to the SENCO about concentration and task completion. In this way, a coherent approach is achieved and everyone on the staff is working towards the same goals.

The use of such a sheet is also valuable for liaising with the SENCO about the type and frequency of support that is required for a particular pupil within a science setting. IEPs are also a useful link with the TA who supports the pupil within the science lesson and can link generic targets to specific situations.

The science teacher may be asked to suggest specific science-related targets for IEPs or as part of other target setting systems, and this is an opportunity to be seized upon. Remember that targets need to be specific and measurable: 'to improve in practical work' is too vague, as is 'to work in a group'. Listed below are some suggestions which can be adapted for use by the science department. (The list of practical competencies in Appendix 7.2 may also be useful.) All of these targets can be evidenced by the teacher or TA and kept in a folder to show progress. Digital photos can be powerful in providing such evidence; for example, take a photograph of a pupil standing next to her set-up experiment and annotate it with details of her achievement: *'Amandeep collected the apparatus for looking at insulators and conductors. She used the list provided and followed the instructions given to set up the investigation without any help.'* This provides clear evidence of attainment and progress and is highly motivating for pupils (use some for display).

IEP targets with a science focus

To be able to:

- collect apparatus for a practical investigation

- set up apparatus for a practical investigation

- observe a practical investigation and comment on what has happened

- record the results from a practical investigation

- name and spell five/six/ten items of science apparatus

- clear away apparatus after a practical investigation

- set up a practical investigation with a partner, following instructions from the teacher/TA

- remember and put into action two/three/four instructions

- stay in seat and 'on task' for ten minutes without intervention

- complete homework set for one week and hand it in on time

- answer correctly a question relating to the practical investigation

- explain how to test for an acid or alkali, or discuss what seeds need to grow, or explain how to separate mixtures, and demonstrate understanding of what makes a 'fair test'.

Case study 8 – Bhavini, Year 9 (visual impairment)

Bhavini has very limited vision and she uses a stick around school. Some pupils have made hurtful comments to her about this. To enhance her sight she has to wear very thick lens glasses, which she hates. She often recognises people by their voices. Outside school she is an active member of the Phab Club (a club for physically handicapped as well as able-bodied teenagers). She goes on outings with them and plays sport but does not like sport in school.

Bhavini has in-class support but wants to be independent around school and so refuses help at the change-over of lessons. The key TA will enlarge work for her and photocopy work to rearrange it in a more visually friendly way; sometimes she will record information and homework instructions onto tape. Bhavini has her own personal tape player with headphones. She always carries a magnifying sheet and has access to a CCTV. She can read Braille.

How can the science teacher support Bhavini?

- Allow her to sit sideways to the teacher so that she can easily hear both the teacher and the rest of the group.

- Ensure lighting is good.

- Avoid standing with your back to the window; this makes it harder for Bhavini to see you.

- If using a textbook, ensure that Bhavini has one of her own.

- Be aware that she may tire easily.

- Use adapted equipment such as talking scales and have a thermistor attached to a buzzer for measuring when containers are full. (The LA VI service will be able to help out with this. The RNIB is also a useful source of information).

- Label apparatus stores in Braille as well as words.

- Use descriptive language.

UNIT: Energy and Electricity   **LESSON: 8**

Lesson Objective (We Are Learning To . . .) Describe how electricity is generated.	IEP Target ● To make greater use of the CCTV.
Learning Outcomes (What I'm Looking For . . .) **ALL** should be able to describe how electricity can be made by a motion between a coil and a magnet. **MOST** should be able to explain how this movement can be caused by burning a fossil fuel. **SOME** will be able to describe the implications of the fact that electricity can't be stored easily.	Key Words electricity, generator, power station

LESSON PLAN	APPARATUS/RESOURCES
Entry Activity Crossword based on fossil fuels.	**Adaptations needed for SEN:**
Starter Ask them to work in groups and in 5 sentences explain where electricity comes from to power a computer. Draw together some of the answers and write these on the board.	● Bhavini's group to record their sentences on a tape recorder as well as writing them on paper, but Bhavini asked to read one sentence the group has recorded. The blinds will need to be closed so that Bhavini can see the light on the dynamo.
Main Demonstrate a bicycle dynamo. Show that as more energy is provided, there is a greater output. Show a video about generating electricity in power stations which use a range of different fuels. Draw flow diagrams to show how the energy stored in the fuel is transferred to leave ultimately as electricity. In groups, use kits to make a generator which will light a light bulb and describe how these work.	● Have an enlarged worksheet to be used with the CCTV for her with the key ideas from the video, she is to circle the key points as she hears them; this will need planning before the lesson.
Extension Research how pumped-storage power stations are used to provide electricity at peak times.	● Bhavini's group to make their generator sound a buzzer rather than light a bulb.
Plenary (Assessment) Use mini-whiteboards to answer a series of questions based on the energy transfer at various stages in the process of the generation of electricity.	
Homework	

Evaluation of the Lesson:

Bhavini was able to read out a sentence using the CCTV but she found it difficult to see the light on the dynamo, although she heard the buzzer with her group's generator. Others enjoyed taping their ideas and it was easy for her to become more involved with the group for this section of the lesson. The worksheet worked well and needs to be stored for future use.

Bibliography

Allan, J. (1995) 'How are we doing? Teachers' views on the effectiveness of co-operative teaching', *Support for Learning*, **10** (3), 127–131.

AQA (2003) *Setting the Standard.* Manchester: AQA.

Ausubel, D. P. (1968) *Educational Psychology: A Cognitive View.* London: Holt, Rinehart and Winston, Inc.

Ayers, H., Clarke, D. and Murray, A. (1998) *Perspectives on Behaviour.* London: David Fulton Publishers.

Beck, A. T. (1989) *Cognitive Therapy and the Emotional Disorders.* London: Penguin.

Bloom, B. S. (1976) *Taxonomy of Educational Objectives*, vol. 1. London: Longman.

Booth, T., *et al.* (2000) *Index for Inclusion.* Bristol: CSIE.

Burns, R. B. (1995) 'Paradigms for research on teaching', in Anderson, L. W. (ed.), *International Encyclopaedia of Teaching and Teacher Education*, 2nd edition. Oxford: Pergamon Press.

Carrol, S. and McQuade, P. (1984) *The Vocational Preparation Manual.* London: Framework Press.

Cattell, R. B. (1931) 'The assessment of teaching ability', *British Journal of Psychology*, **1**, 48–72.

CLEAPPS (1997) *School Science Service.* London: CLEAPPS.

Collins, N. (1986) *New Teaching Skills.* Oxford: Oxford University Press.

Cooper, P., Smith, C. J. and Upton, G. (1994) *Emotional and Behavioural Difficulties: Theory to Practice.* London: Routledge.

Cowne, E. A. (2003) *The SENCO Handbook* (4th edn). London: David Fulton Publishers.

DfEE (2000) *Working with Teaching Assistants.* London: DfEE Publications.

DfEE (2001) *Schools Achieving Success.* Norwich: HMSO.

DfEE (2001) *Schools Building on Success.* Norwich: HMSO.

DfES (2001) *Special Educational Needs Code of Practice.* London: DfES Publications.

DfES (2002) *Key Stage 3 National Strategy: Launch of the Science Strand in Special Schools and Units.* London: DfES Publications.

DfES (2002) *National Strategy for Key Stage 3.* London: DfES Publications.

DfES (2004) *Removing Barriers to Achievement: The Government's Strategy for SEN.* London: DfES.

Farrell, M. (1998) *The Special Education Handbook.* London: David Fulton Publishers.

Fogell, J. and Long, R. (1997) *Emotional and Behavioural Difficulties.* Tamworth: NASEN.

Gagne, R. N. (1965) *Learning and Individual Differences.* Columbus, OH: Charles E. Merrill Publishing Company.

Gardner, H. (1993) *Frames of Mind: Theory of Multiple Intelligences.* London: Fontana Press.

Gardner, H. (2000) *Intelligence Reframed: Multiple Intelligences for the 21st Century.* New York: Basic Books.

Gordon, R. (1996) *The Primary Behaviour File.* London: David Fulton Publishers.

Hewett, D. (1998) *Challenging Behaviour.* London: David Fulton Publishers.

Kyriacou, C. (1997) *Effective Teaching in Schools: Theory and Practice.* Cheltenham: Stanley Thomas Ltd.

Kyriacou, C. (2001) *Essential Teaching Skills.* Cheltenham: Stanley Thomas Ltd.

Levesley, M., Baggley, S., Clark, J., *et al.* (2002) *Exploring Science.* Essex: Longman.

LGNTO (2001) *Teaching/Classroom Assistants National Occupational Standards.* London: Local Government National Training Organisation.

Lovey, J. (1995) *Supporting Special Educational Needs in Secondary School Classrooms.* London: David Fulton Publishers in association with the Roehampton Institute.

Margerison, A. (1997) 'Class teachers and the role of classroom assistants in the delivery of special educational needs', *Support for Learning* 12(4), 166–169.

Marvin, C. and Stokoe, C. (2003) *Access to Science: Curriculum Planning and Practical Activities for Pupils with Learning Difficulties.* London: David Fulton Publishers.

McNamara, S. and Moreton, G. (1997) *Understanding Differentiation.* London: David Fulton Publishers.

McNamara, S. and Moreton, G. (1999) *Changing Behaviour.* London: David Fulton Publishers.

Moore, J. (2002) 'The role of observation in teacher appraisal', in Tilstone, C. (ed.) *Observing Teaching and Learning.* London: David Fulton Publishers.

Ofsted (2002) *The Key Stage 3 Strategy: Evaluation of the First Year of the Pilot.* Ofsted: London.

Ofsted (2003) *Special Educational Needs in the Mainstream.* London: Ofsted.

Piaget, J. (1972) *Psychology and Epistemology.* Harmondsworth: Penguin.

Portwood, M. (1999) *Developmental Dyspraxia.* London: David Fulton Publishers.

Postman, N. and Weingartner, C. (1969) *Teaching as a Subversive Activity.* Harmondsworth: Penguin.

QCA (2000) *Science: A Scheme of Work for Key Stage 3.* London: QCA.

QCA (2001) *Science: Planning, Teaching and Assessing the Curriculum for Pupils with Learning Difficulties.* London: QCA.

Rogers, B. (1997) *Cracking the Hard Class.* Sydney: Scholastic.

Rogers, D. (1969) *Child Psychology.* Belmont, CA: Brookes and Cole.

Sang, D. and Wood-Robinson, V. (2002) *Teaching Secondary Scientific Enquiry.* London: ASE and John Murray.

Skinner, B. F. (1993) *About Behaviourism.* London: Penguin.

Sotto, E. (1997) *When Teaching Becomes Learning: A Theory and Practice of Teaching.* London: Cassell.

Stakes, R. and Hornby, G. (2000) *Meeting Special Needs in Mainstream Schools*, 2nd edn. London: David Fulton Publishers.

Warnock, M. (chair) (1978) *Special Educational Needs: Report of the Committee of Enquiry into the Education of Handicapped Children and Young People (The Warnock Report)*. London: HMSO.

Welding, J. (1996) 'In-class support: A successful way of meeting individual student need?' *Support for Learning* 11(3), 113–17.

Winnicott, D. (1991) *The Child, the Family and the Outside World*. Harmondsworth: Penguin.

Resources and Useful Websites

ASE resources:

Games (multiple choice, crosswords, etc.): www.ase.org.uk/sen/focus/hot-potato.htm

Mr Zippy's Trainers: www.ase.org.uk/sen/focus/mr-zippy.htm

Odd One Out: www.ase.org.uk/sen/words/odd-one-out.htm

Rainforest with Symbols: www.ase.org.uk/sen/words/rainforest.htm

Rocket project: www.ase.org.uk/sen/further/case-studies.htm

Running person: www.ase.org.uk/sen/focus/muscles.htm

Crick Software (Clicker, ClozePro, Find Out and Write About)

Crick House

Boarden Close

Moulton Park

Northampton NN3 6LF

Tel: 01604 671 691, fax: 01604 671 692

email: info@cricksoft.com, website: www.cricksoft.com

Digital microscope:

www.sycd.co.uk/primary/ict/cameras-and-microscopes.htm

General advice for ICT, SEN and inclusion:

www.ictadvice.org.uk/index.php?section=tl&rid-2345&catcode=as_inc_sup_03

Inclusive science main website:

www.issen.org.uk

Make your own world:

www.sycd.co.uk/is_there_life/p10/activity.htm

Nottingham Rehab (products for occupational therapy and rehabilitation)

Findel House

Excelsior Road

Ashby Park

Ashby de la Zouch

Leicestershire LE65 1NG

Telephone: 0845 606 0911, fax: 01530 419 150

Website: www.nrs-uk.co.uk

INSET Activity: Main Points of SENDA

1. The SEN and Disability Act 2001 amends the Disability Discrimination Act 1995 to include schools' and LEAs' responsibility to provide for pupils and students with disabilities.

2. The definition of a disability in this Act is:

   'someone who has a physical or mental impairment that has an effect on his or her ability to carry out normal day to day activities. The effect must be:

   - substantial (that is, more than minor or trivial); and

   - long term (that is, has lasted or is likely to last for at least a year or for the rest of the life of the person affected); and

   - adverse.'

Activity: List any pupils that you come across that would fall in to this category.

3. The Act states that the responsible body for a school must take such steps as it is reasonable to take to ensure that disabled pupils and disabled prospective pupils are not placed at substantial disadvantage in comparison with those who are not disabled.

Activity: Give an example of something which might be considered 'a substantial disadvantage'.

4. The duty on the school to make reasonable adjustments is anticipatory. This means that a school should not wait until a disabled pupil seeks admission to consider what adjustments it might make generally to meet the needs of disabled pupils.

Activity: Think of two reasonable adjustments that could be made in your school/ department.

5. The school has a duty to plan strategically for increasing access to the school education. This includes provision of information for pupils and parents (e.g. Braille or taped versions of brochures), improving the physical environment for disabled students and increasing access to the curriculum by further differentiation.

Activity: Consider ways of increasing access to the school for a pupil requesting admission who has Down syndrome with low levels of literacy and a heart condition that affects strenuous physical activity.

6. Schools need to be proactive in seeking out information about a pupil's disability (by establishing good relationships with parents and carers, asking about disabilities during admission interviews, etc.) and ensuring that all staff who might come across the pupil are aware of the pupil's disability.

Activity: List the opportunities that occur in your school for staff to gain information about disabled students. How can these be improved on?

INSET Activity: What Do We Really Think?

Each member of the department should choose two of these statements and pin them up on the noticeboard for an overview of staff opinion. The person leading the session (head of department, SENCO, senior manager) should be ready to address any negative feedback and take forward the department in a positive approach.

Children with more severe problems will get no benefit from studying science and will just hold other children back.

Statemented children are the SENCO's responsibility and should be concentrating on basic skills instead of learning about science.

Experiments are great for every pupil. We can devise a lot of activities that are not reliant on good reading and writing skills.

Some pupils are only interested in playing games and there's no point in teaching them anything else.

I want to be able to cater for pupils with SEN and would find it beneficial to work with an expert in SEN.

Science opens up new worlds, and that is as true for pupils who have limited language or sensory impairments.

You can't trust some youngsters with digital cameras. They'll break them.

If their behaviour distracts other pupils in any way, youngsters with SEN should be withdrawn from the class.

Are we covered in insurance if they take cameras or other equipment outside? Can we trust some of these pupils to bring them back?

Children need to learn about science. It's an important part of understanding the world around us.

I need much more time to plan if pupils with SEN are going to be coming to my lessons.

I have enough to do working out the strategy for science without worrying about pupils who can barely read or write.

Key Words for a Unit on Electricity

Word	Meaning
Ammeter	a device which measures the size of electric current in a circuit
Ampere (amp)	the unit of electric current
Cell	a device which transfers energy when connected in a circuit
Current (electric)	the rate of flow of electricity in a circuit
Electron	the tiny particle, with a negative charge, flowing around a circuit
Parallel circuit	a circuit which divides, so electricity has a choice of routes, before it joins up again
Resistor	a component that makes the flow of electricity more difficult
Series circuit	a circuit where components are arranged so that electricity flows through each one in turn before returning to the cell
Volt	the unit used to measure the push of the electricity in a circuit
Voltmeter	a device for measuring the push of electricity in a circuit

SEN Training for Science Staff

Some questions to consider when creating an inclusive learning environment

- What is it like to live with certain disabilities?
- How does each of these affect the student's ability to carry out simple experiments?
- How can we modify the laboratory to help these students?
- How do we modify teaching materials to support these students?
- How do we modify apparatus to support these students?
- Do we need any other apparatus or resources?

Simulating disabilities

It is rarely possible to simulate disabilities so that your experience is exactly the same as the student's. Coping with a disability for a short period is completely different from coping with this every day of your life. However, it makes us more aware if we simulate and try to experience these difficulties.

Visual impairment

Wrap cling film or bubble wrap unevenly round a pair of goggles to restrict the vision.

Now set up a microscope and dissect a flower, look at the anthers and observe the pollen grains.

How did you feel?

YOU HAVE TO DO EVERYTHING WEARING THE GOGGLES.

Physical disabilities

Bind your index and middle fingers together on both hands.

Now collect and test the pH of 3 solutions with pH paper.

Now do the same but use a pH meter

Which method was the easier?

Hearing impairment

Make a tape with low-level background noise, such as running water, music, etc., and the occasional loud noise, and over the top of this give some verbal instructions.

Ask another member of your department to listen to the tape and write the instructions down.

Collect the following feedback:

- How easy was it to write the instructions down?

- Which of the noises caused most distraction?

- How could you make it easier for this student to receive these instructions?

Summing up

- What were the difficulties you encountered?

- How could these have been overcome to make access to the science better?

- How could we improve access to the curriculum for our pupils with SEN?

Worksheet – Stopping Rust

Name: date: class:

You need to collect:	
4 iron nails	salt water
4 test tubes (numbered 1–4)	paint
grease	strips of zinc

What to do:

1. paint one nail and let it dry
2. put grease on the second nail
3. wrap a strip of zinc around the third nail
4. the last nail can be used as it is
5. put the test tubes into a rack and put one nail in each

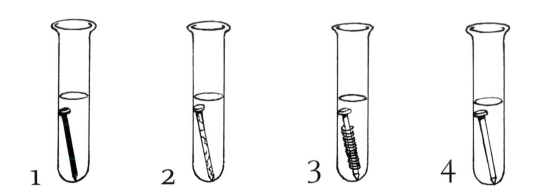

1   2   3   4

6. pour salt water into the test tubes to cover the nails
7. leave the test tubes for a week then look to see what has happened.

Write down your results

Nail:	What the nail looks like after one week in the salt water:
1. painted	
2. greased	
3. zinc covered	
4. untreated	

What does this show?

Which is the best way to stop iron from going rusty?

Writing Frame 1 Planning an Investigation

This is the apparatus I will need:	
This is what I will do:	
This is what I will do to make the experiment a fair test:	
This is what I will do to make it safe:	

If I change.., the variable, my prediction will be:
Prediction: What I think will happen is:
This is because:

By using Clicker, some phrases could be put in the boxes and then the pupil will only have to move them by clicking on them.

Presenting My Results

Now I have my results, how will I present them?
I could draw a pie chart like this one using my results.
I will need to give it a title and label the parts.

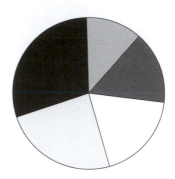

I could draw a bar chart like this with my results. I will need to label the axes.

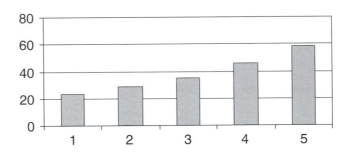

I could draw a line graph. I will need to give it a title and label the axes.

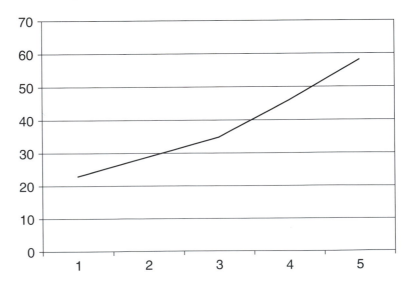

When I draw graphs the thing I alter (the variable) goes along the bottom axis.

Speaking Frame – A Science Experiment

This is an account of an experiment to see

. . . .

. . . .

The equipment required was

. . . .

. . . .

The procedure was as follows:

. . . .

. . . .

Explain the procedure using time connectives, e.g.

First …………… **Next** ……………

Then …………… **Meanwhile** ……………

Eventually ……………

Use impersonal language and the passive voice, e.g.

… **were placed**

… **were observed**

… **was noted**

It was expected that ……………………………………………………………………..

Our findings were that ………………………………………………………………..

This suggests that ………………………………………………………………………

(Used with permission from Palmer, S. (2004) *Speaking Frames: Year 6*. London: David Fulton Publishers.)

This is an account of an experiment to see *whether evaporation of water is affected by the temperature.*

The equipment required was *three squares of thick card (all the same size), three plastic trays, a stopwatch, a digital thermometer and a bucket of water.*

The procedure was as follows:

First, the squares of card were all dipped in the bucket for 10 seconds, to ensure that they absorbed the same amount of water. They were then placed in the plastic trays, and kept at different temperatures: one in the bottom of a fridge, one in a cool outdoor shed and the third in a warm room. The temperature of each location was checked with the digital thermometer. Then the cards were checked at 10-minute intervals to see if they were dry.

It was expected that *the card in the warm position would dry first.*

Our findings were that *the card kept in the warm classroom (22°C) dried after 40 minutes; the card in the cool shed (11°C) took 3 hours 50 minutes to dry, and the card in the refrigerator (2°C) was still wet after 6 hours.*

This suggests that temperature affects the speed at which water evaporates – the warmer it is, the faster evaporation occurs.

Number Line and Temperature Change

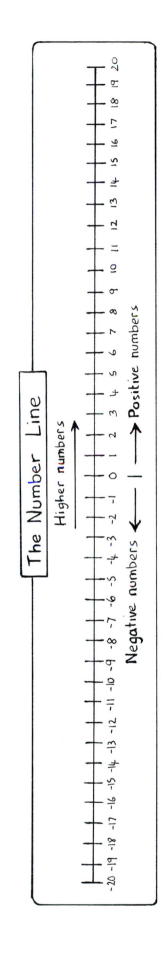

The Number Line

Higher numbers

Negative numbers ← | → Positive numbers

-20 -19 -18 -17 -16 -15 -14 -13 -12 -11 -10 -9 -8 -7 -6 -5 -4 -3 -2 -1 0 1 2 3 4 5 6 7 8 9 10 11 12 13 14 15 16 17 18 19 20

The temperature in the freezer was −15°C but it rose to 7°C when there was a power cut. What was the rise in temperature? Mark the numbers and count between them.

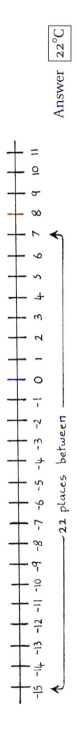

-15 -14 -13 -12 -11 -10 -9 -8 -7 -6 -5 -4 -3 -2 -1 0 1 2 3 4 5 6 7 8 9 10 11

22 places between

Answer 22°C

Keeping a Tally

This is a quick way to record something happening – or seconds ticking by:

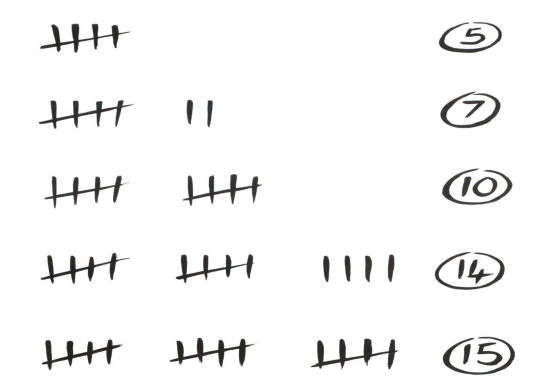

Types of Numbers

Types of Numbers

numerator

$$\frac{3}{4} = 0.75 = 75\%$$

denominator

percentage

decimal

Multiplication – Times Tables

x	1	2	3	4	5	6	7	8	9	10
1	1	2	3	4	5	6	7	8	9	10
2	2	4	6	8	10	12	14	16	18	20
3	3	6	9	12	15	18	21	24	27	30
4	4	8	12	16	20	24	28	32	36	40
5	5	10	15	20	25	30	35	40	45	50
6	6	12	18	24	30	36	42	48	54	60
7	7	14	21	28	35	42	49	56	63	70
8	8	16	24	32	40	48	56	64	72	80
9	9	18	27	36	45	54	63	72	81	90
10	10	20	30	40	50	60	70	80	90	100

Time

The clock

Twenty past eight – 8.20 pm (evening) or 20.20 hrs.

Digital display

or

24 hours in a day

60 minutes in an hour

60 seconds in a minute

Measuring

Length, height, distance

millimetre   (mm)
centimetre   (cm)
metre   (m)
kilometre   (km)

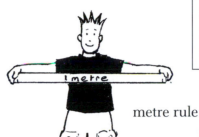

metre rule

(one metre is a bit more
than 3 feet)

| 1 cm = 10 mm |
| 1 m = 100 cm |
| 1 km = 1000 m |

Mass

gram   (g)
kilogram   (kg/kilo)

| 1 kilo = 1000 g |

(one kilo is a bit more
than 2 pounds)

Liquids

millilitre   (ml)
litre   (l)

| 1 litre = 1000 ml |

(one litre is a bit less
than 2 pints)

Thermometers measure temperature

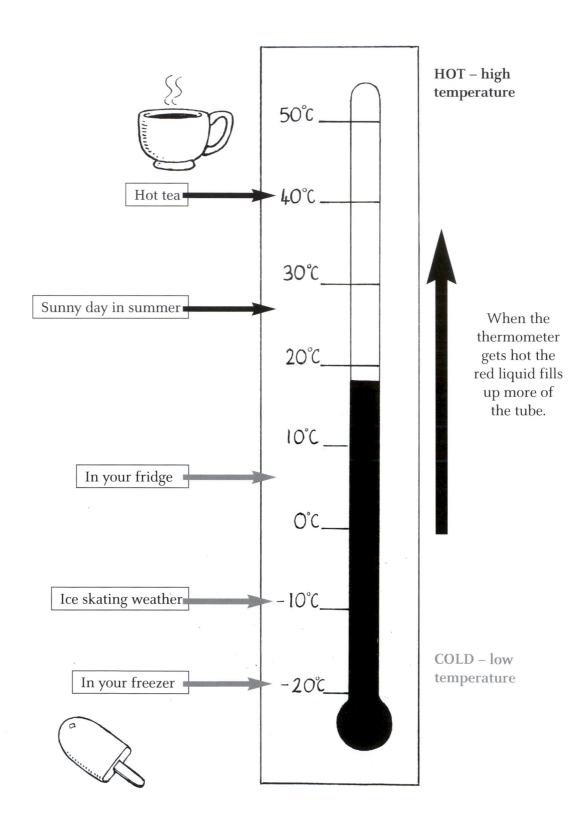

HOT – high temperature

Hot tea

50°C

40°C

30°C

Sunny day in summer

20°C

When the thermometer gets hot the red liquid fills up more of the tube.

10°C

In your fridge

0°C

Ice skating weather

-10°C

COLD – low temperature

In your freezer

-20°C

Boiling and Freezing

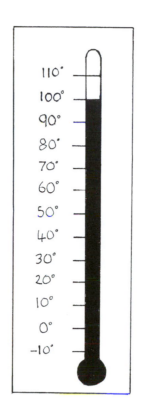

1. *Heating* water to 100°C makes it *boil*. When water boils it turns into steam

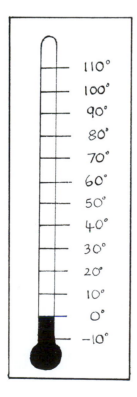

2. *Cooling* water to 0°C or below makes it *freeze*. When it's frozen it's completely *solid* – ice

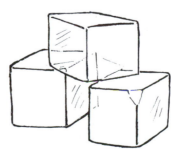

Conductors and Insulators – Heat Energy

1) Some materials let heat energy pass through them easily

1. These materials are called *THERMAL CONDUCTORS*.
2. *METALS* are good *THERMAL CONDUCTORS*.
3. Because heat energy passes through them quickly metals normally feel *COLD*.

Energy

2) Some materials do not let heat energy pass through them

1. Materials that do not let heat energy pass through them are called *THERMAL INSULATORS*.

| Cork pot stand | Wooden handle | Oven glove | Thermal vest |

2. Plastic, cork, wood and fabrics are good *THERMAL INSULATORS*.
3. Thermal insulators are good for keeping heat *OUT* as well as *IN*.

| Cool box | Thermos | Polystyrene cup |

Used to keep food cool   Used to keep hot drinks hot – and cold drinks cold.

A _GOOD INSULATOR_ = A _POOR CONDUCTOR_

Conductors and Insulators – Electricity

1) Conductors let electricity flow through them

1. Materials that can carry electricity are called *conductors* – they *conduct* electricity.
2. *Metals* such as copper, iron, steel and aluminium are all good conductors.

2) Insulators do not let electricity flow through them

1. Materials that *cannot* carry electricity are called *insulators* – they don't conduct electricity.
2. Wood, plastic, glass and rubber are all insulators.

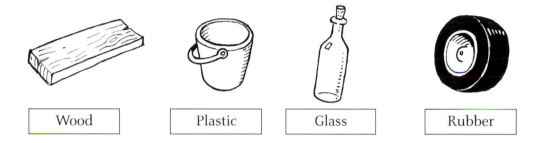

| Wood | Plastic | Glass | Rubber |

3) Insulators and conductors both have important uses

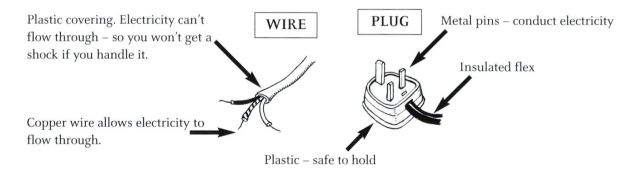

Plastic covering. Electricity can't flow through – so you won't get a shock if you handle it.

WIRE

PLUG

Metal pins – conduct electricity

Insulated flex

Copper wire allows electricity to flow through.

Plastic – safe to hold

4) Electricity can be dangerous

You shouldn't touch *anything* electrical with wet hands – and that includes *switches*. Electricity can be conducted through sweat (salty water) to your body, giving you an electric shock.

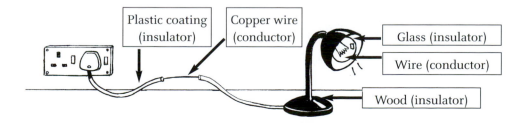

Plastic coating (insulator)

Copper wire (conductor)

Glass (insulator)

Wire (conductor)

Wood (insulator)

Reading Scales

exactly 900 ml of liquid

The level is <u>between</u> 40 ml and 50 ml. The lines between 40 ml and 50 ml divide into 5 equal portions – so each must be 2 ml. 42, 44, 46, 48 ml. The liquid is up to the third line from 40 so count in 2's

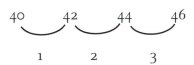

There are 46 ml of liquid

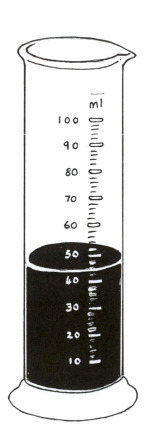

Graphs

The graph shows the temperature of water in a kettle over 2 minutes.

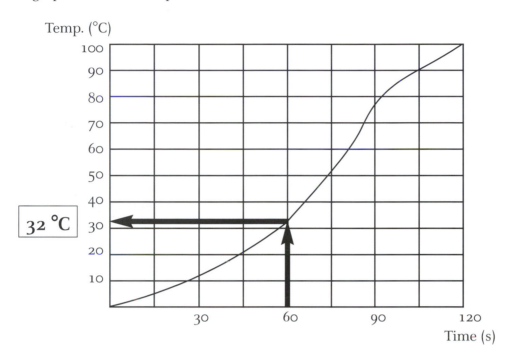

Question: What is the temperature of the water after 60 seconds?

To find out:

1. Find the 60 s mark on the bottom axis and draw a line upwards (vertical) until it meets the graph line.

2. Draw a line across (horizontal) to the side axis.

3. Read the value (temperature on the side axis). The answer is: 32°c

Clicker Grids

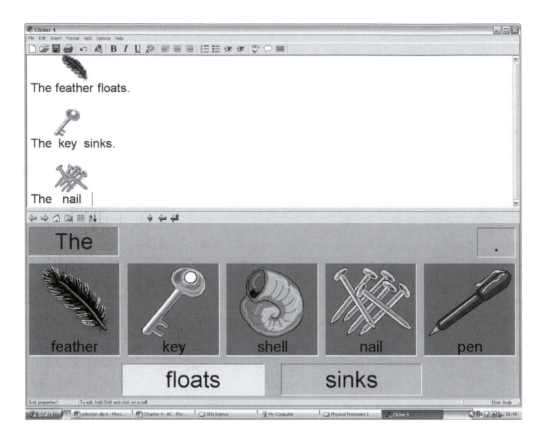

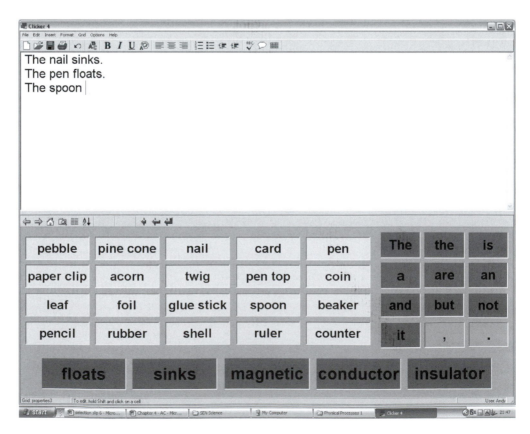

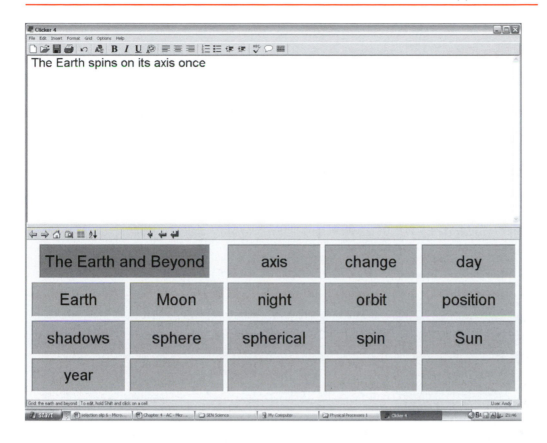

ClozePro

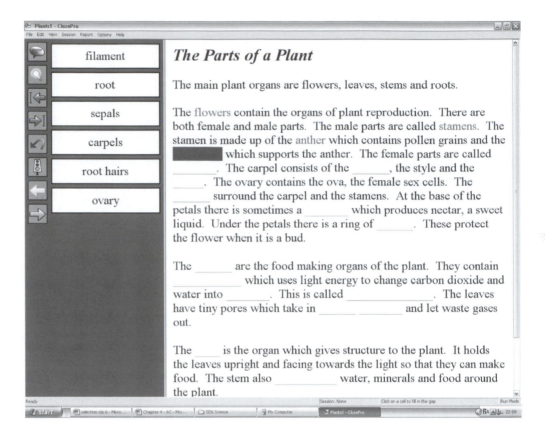

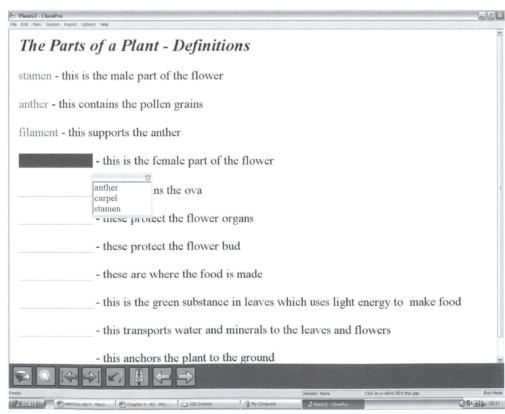

Plants4 - ClozePro

File   Edit   View   Session   Report   Options   Help

The Parts of a Plant - Spelling

stamen - this is the male part of the flower

ca|*** - this is the female part of the flower

petals - these protect the flower organs

leaves - these are where the food is made

stem - this transports water and minerals to the leaves and flowers

root - this anchors the plant to the ground

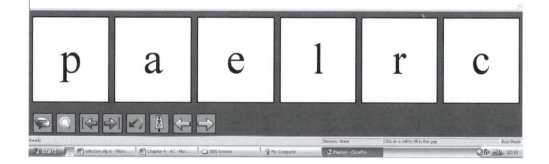

Ready   Session: None   Click on a cell to fill in the gap   Run Mode

Start | selection slip 6 - Micro... | Chapter 4 - AC - Micr... | SEN Science | My Computer | Plants4 - ClozePro | 22:10

Key Words and Diagrams for a Unit on Electricity

A simple circuit

Cell (a source of electrical energy)

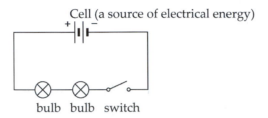

Bulb

This is a series circuit

Cell (a source of electrical energy)

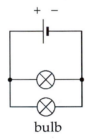

bulb   bulb   switch

This is a parallel circuit

Cell (a source of electricity)

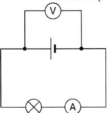

bulb

Measuring current and voltage

Voltmeter (measures voltage, the push of electricity)

bulb   Ammeter (measures current, the rate of flow of electricity)

Starter Activity – Tug of War

Example activity using a picture as a stimulus

The picture above shows a tug of war match the two sides are quite evenly matched. For the first two minutes of the match, even though both teams are pulling as hard as they can, the rope doesn't move. After two minutes, one of the sides just has the edge and they slowly pull the rope and win the match.

Describe this tug of war match by explaining what happens to the forces involved. Use as many of these words as possible:

- Pull
- Balanced
- Unbalanced
- Tension
- Friction
- Accelerate
- Stationary

SMOG Test for Readability

SMOG Ready Reckoner

1	Select a text	
2	Count 10 sentences	
3	Count number of words which have three or more syllables	
4	Multiply this by 3	

5 Circle the number closest to your answer

1   4   9   16   25   36   49   64   81

100   121   144   169

6 Find the square root of the number you circled

1	4	9	16	25	36	49	64	81	100	121	144	169
1	2	3	4	5	6	7	8	9	10	11	12	13

7 Add 8   Readability level

The lower the readability level the easier something is to read and understand. A readability level under about 10 will be able to be understood by most people.

Homework Activity

Homework activity 1 – Learning key words

How the body is protected against disease

Draw a line between the correct word and definition.

Scab	When blood becomes solid. Makes a 'scab' when it is on the surface of the skin.
Mucus	A strong chemical used to kill microbes.
Clot	Chemicals made by some white blood cells. They attach themselves to microbes and destroy them.
Disinfectant	A sticky liquid that traps microbes and dust in the nose and trachea.
White blood cell	A dry clot of blood on the surface of the skin.
Antibody	A blood cell which helps to kill microbes. They can surround the microbe or make chemicals that kill it.

Homework Activity 2 – Research

Letter from an alien

Imagine you are an alien from one of the planets and you are writing to your friend on Earth. Include all the planets you have travelled to, saying what they are like.

Dear ....,

I am your friend, ..., the alien. Your planet Earth is very pleasant because . . . .
. . . .

I first visited Mercury but I did not like it because it was . . . .
. . . .

Next I went to Venus, that was pretty because . . . .
. . . .

Then I went to Mars. I wouldn't like to live there because . . . .
. . . .

My space ship then took me to Jupiter, this has . . . .
. . . .

Even though I was missing home, I continued with my journey and went to Saturn. This planet has . . . .
. . . .

The next planet I flew to was Uranus. This was .... miles from the Sun.

Neptune has a few interesting features like . . . .
. . . .

Finally I landed on Pluto. It took ages to get to this planet, but I did not like it because . . . .
. . . .

Homework Activity 3 –Writing up an Experiment

Testing for microbes

The apparatus I used was:

An a _ _ _   p_ _ _ _
A wire loop
Sticky t _ _ _
A b _ _ _ _ _   b _ _ _ _ _

My method was:

I put the wire loop into the f _ _ _ _ until it was hot.

(I did this so that . . . .

. . . .)

I dipped the wire loop into the bottle of culture.

I made lines gently on the a _ _ _   p_ _ _ _ with the wire loop.

I put the top on the a _ _ _   p _ _ _ _ and sealed it with sticky t _ _ _.

I then put it in an oven at _ _ °C and left it for 2 days.

(I did this so that . . . .

. . . .

. . . .)

The 5-Star Lesson Plan

❖ Clear learning objectives set for the lesson.

❖ Consideration to the ability of the pupils; setting attainable but high expectations.

❖ The lesson content planned to suit the learning styles of the pupils. This is very important for pupils with SEN. Do not use the same format every time. The lesson could contain:

- Introduction
- Main teaching activity
- Plenary.

❖ Clearly defined method of monitoring progress.

❖ Evaluation of the lesson for future use.

TA Strengths and Areas for Development in Science

Name . . . .

Consider your work within the science faculty

In the following self-assessment procedure, 5 is most effective and 1 is least effective.

1. How do you rate your awareness of the faculty's policies and procedures?

    1 2 3 4 5

2. Underline the areas of science you feel most confident with

    biology/chemistry/physics/all

3. What do you consider to be your areas of strength?

    Working with individual pupils   1 2 3 4 5
    Working with groups of pupil   1 2 3 4 5
    Working within a wholeclass setting   1 2 3 4 5
    Collaborating with teaching staff   1 2 3 4 5
    Working with pupils with particular special
    educational need (specify type of need) 1 2 3 4 5
    Making differentiated worksheets   1 2 3 4 5
    Supporting pupils with literacy   1 2 3 4 5
    Supporting pupils with numeracy   1 2 3 4 5
    Other: . . . .

4. Do you have any particular training needs within science?

. . . .
. . . .
. . . .
. . . .

Please add additional comments you feel are important.

. . . .
. . . .
. . . .
. . . .

Training for Teaching Assistants Working in the Science Faculty

You need to know the school/science faculty policies on:

- safety
- behaviour
- homework
- assessment and monitoring.

You will need to know how to:

- light a Bunsen burner
- heat a test tube in a Bunsen flame
- heat a beaker of water
- use a measuring cylinder
- use a balance
- use a thermometer
- use a retort stand
- use a stop clock
- filter a mixture
- evaporate a liquid
- set up a simple electrical circuit
- use an ammeter, voltmeter and variable resistor
- take a pulse
- find the pH of a substance.

Other useful skills include:

- how to draw a graph or bar chart from data collected
- how to use a datalogger
- how to draw a graph using a computer.

Medium-Term Planning – Termly

Term Autumn/Spring/Summer   **Year Group** . . . .

Date	Unit	Key words	Practicals	Adaptations for SEN pupil	Assessments

Short-Term Planning – Weekly

Teaching Group . . . .

Date	Lesson	Key words	Worksheet needed	Equipment needed	Use of support
	1				
Adaptations needed					
	2				
Adaptations needed					
	3				
Adaptations needed					
	4				
Adaptations needed					

TA Planning Sheet for Science Lessons

Science Group . . . .   Unit . . . .

Pupil(s) Needing Support . . . .

Date	Lesson	Objectives	Key words	Adaptations/differentiation required
	1			
	2			
	3			
	4			
	5			
	6			
	7			
	8			
	9			
	10			

Additional notes:

Lesson Plan – Food and Digestion

UNIT: Food and Digestion   **LESSON: 4**

Lesson Objective (We Are Learning To . . .) Describe how the size of the food particles is important for absorption.	IEP Targets • To complete the written work set for the lesson. • Put up hand when answering questions.
Learning Outcomes (What I'm Looking For . . .) **ALL** should be able to describe that starch, protein and fat molecules are too big to be absorbed. **MOST** should explain how these larger particles can be broken down into smaller ones. **SOME** will be able to explain this using the idea of the sizes of hole in the wall of the small intestines.	**Key Words** Digestion, molecule, starch, sugar, small intestine

LESSON PLAN	APPARATUS/RESOURCES

Entry Activity
Place pictures of different foods into groups to show which of the food groups they are rich in.
 	
Starter
Split the class into 4 groups with a model torso or large diagram each. Question and answer session: if a member of the group gets a question right, they place a digestive organ on the torso/diagram. The winning group is the first one with a complete digestive system.
 	
Main
Start by sorting large and small building blocks through holes; use the results of this to predict whether large starch molecules will be able to pass through the wall of the intestines.
   Class practical with starch and glucose solution inside Visking tubing, placed in a beaker of water.
   Test the water from the beaker for starch and glucose every 5 minutes for 20 minutes.
   Write an explanation of their findings, again using the building blocks as a model to help with this.
 	
Plenary (Assessment)
Information cards on proteins and amino acids, use these to explain which will pass through the wall of the intestines. Discuss in groups and feedback to the rest of the class.
 	
Homework
	Adaptations needed for SEN:
	• This lesson contains many opportunities for Steven to take turns. The writing is also broken up into smaller units to enable him and others in the group to cope with the written work expected.
	• Before Steven begins his practical work, he has to write a risk assessment of the lesson and have it checked.
	• Steven is encouraged to use key words on cards as a method of organising his thoughts. The TA is present but working with another group of students who need support with the practical work.

Evaluation of the Lesson:

It would have been useful to have a worksheet with practical instructions for Steven as he found it difficult to remember all of the details. He needed four reminders to put his hand up during the lesson.

   He did not have to leave the room owing to poor behaviour in this lesson.

Lesson Plan – Energy and Electricity

UNIT: Energy and Electricity   **LESSON:** 8

Lesson Objective (We Are Learning To . . .) Describe how electricity is generated.	IEP Target • To make greater use of the CCTV.
Learning Outcomes (What I'm Looking For . . .) **ALL** should be able to describe how electricity can be made by a motion between a coil and a magnet. **MOST** should be able to explain how this movement can be caused by burning a fossil fuel. **SOME** will be able to describe the implications of the fact that electricity can't be stored easily.	**Key Words** electricity, generator, power station

LESSON PLAN	APPARATUS/RESOURCES
Entry Activity Crossword based on fossil fuels.	**Adaptations needed for SEN:** • Bhavini's group to record their sentences on a tape recorder as well as writing them on paper, but Bhavini asked to read one sentence the group has recorded. The blinds will need to be closed so that Bhavini can see the light on the dynamo.
Starter Ask them to work in groups and in 5 sentences explain where electricity comes from to power a computer. Draw together some of the answers and write these on the board.	• Have an enlarged worksheet to be used with the CCTV for her with the key ideas from the video, she is to circle the key points as she hears them; this will need planning before the lesson.
Main Demonstrate a bicycle dynamo. Show that as more energy is provided, there is a greater output. Show a video about generating electricity in power stations which use a range of different fuels. Draw flow diagrams to show how the energy stored in the fuel is transferred to leave ultimately as electricity. In groups, use kits to make a generator which will light a light bulb and describe how these work.	• Bhavini's group to make their generator sound a buzzer rather than light a bulb.
Extension Research how pumped-storage power stations are used to provide electricity at peak times.	
Plenary (Assessment) Use mini-whiteboards to answer a series of questions based on the energy transfer at various stages in the process of the generation of electricity.	
Homework	

Evaluation of the Lesson:

Bhavini was able to read out a sentence using the CCTV but she found it difficult to see the light on the dynamo, although she heard the buzzer with her group's generator. Others enjoyed taping their ideas and it was easy for her to become more involved with the group for this section of the lesson. The worksheet worked well and needs to be stored for future use.